ALL FOR ONE

A Play in Two Acts

by Paul Weitz

(Comedy – Drama)

IMPORTANT BILLING AND CREDIT REQUIREMENTS

All producers of ALL FOR ONE *must* give credit to the Author of the Play in all programs distributed in connection with performances of the Play and in all instances in which the title of the Play appears for purposes of advertising, publicizing or otherwise exploiting the Play and/or a production. The name of the Author *must* also appear on a separate line, on which no other name appears, immediately following the title, and *must* appear in size of type not less than fifty percent the size of the title type.

All For One premiered December 2, 1993 at the Ensemble Studio Theatre in New York City, in association with Daniel Selznick, Alexander Racolin and Annette Moskowitz. It was directed by Kate Baggott and had the following cast:

TONY --John Speredakos
LYNN --Calista Flockhart
JEFF-- Liev Schreiber
JONNY LIGHTNINGROD---------------Michael Louis Wells
FARAH---Noelle Parker

Production Stage Manager	Elaine Bayless
Asst. Stage Manager	Mark Roberts
Set Designer	David Gallo
Asst. Set Designer	David Kutos
Costume Designer	Julie Doyle
Lighting Designer	Glen Fasman
Sound Designer	Ephraim Kelman
Props Construction	Sally Plass
Technical Director	Carlo Adinolfi

CHARACTERS

TONY, age 26, is the writer/producer of the hit show, "Model Detectives."

LYNN, age 26, is a teacher. She's beginning to wonder what she's doing in Hollywood.

JEFF, age 26, is a law student. He thinks about thinking.

JONNY LIGHTNINGROD, age 26, is an aspiring rock musician. He's living it.

FARRAH, age 17, would like to improve her lifestyle immediately, at all costs.

TIME & PLACE

The living room of an expensive house in Los Angeles.

The present.

**With thanks to
Tony Connor, Kenneth Pressman
and Larry Pressman**

ALL FOR ONE

Scene 1

DAYLIGHT up, illuminating the living room of a house in Los Angeles. Downstage, facing away from the audience, is a TV with its cord conspicuously unplugged. TONY is lounging on the couch. LYNN is standing behind Tony with her hands on his shoulders. JEFF is sitting in an easy chair, looking uneasy. THEY're all twenty-six years old.

TONY. It's so great to see you.

LYNN. You look exactly the same.

JEFF. (*Disappointed.*) Oh.

LYNN. Tony's getting grey hair.

TONY. At age twenty-six.

JEFF. You must ... think a lot.

TONY. I try not to.

LYNN. And you usually succeed. (*SHE kisses him on the top of his head.*)

TONY. Hey, look what I found in the attic. (*TONY points at the coffee table, which has a board game, Strat-o-matic Baseball, laid out on it.*)

JEFF. What is it?

TONY. What do you mean, what is it? It's Strat-o-matic Baseball!

JEFF. Oh, that uh ... baseball game.

TONY. Remember? Remember? I have old-timer teams. (*TONY picks up some white printed cards.*) Joe DiMaggio! Rogers Hornsby! Frankie Frisch!

JEFF. Hunh.

TONY. I thought you, me and Fred could play a tournament. (*To Lynn.*) After every baseball game we used to come home and play Strat-o. We had a World Series and everything.

LYNN. He might not want to play, Tony.

TONY. Are you kidding? You want to play, don't you Jeff?

JEFF. Uh ...

LYNN. "When I was a child, I spoke as a child, I understood as a child, I thought as a child: but when I became a man, I put away childish things ..."

TONY. Who said that, John Wayne Gacy?

LYNN. It's in the Bible.

TONY. The Bible. Why on earth are you quoting the Bible?

JEFF. "... For now we see through a glass, darkly; but then face to face: now I know in part; but then I shall know even as also I am known."

TONY. So, how was your flight?

JEFF. It was pretty good, I ... threw up.

LYNN. What, in one of those air-sickness bags?

JEFF. No, I made it to the lavatory, but ... other than that it was, you know, a good flight.

TONY. Too bad about your luggage.

JEFF. That's alright, I've always ... wanted to go to Paris. Now if I don't make it, at least I'll know my brown suitcase has been there.

LYNN. Hope the rest of your trip won't be as much of a disaster.

TONY. Wish you were staying longer.

JEFF. I have to get back to my summer job at ... Davis, Davis and Rabinowitz.

TONY. What's that, a law firm?

JEFF. Well ... of course.

(The PHONE rings.)

TONY. I'll get it ... Hello? ... Ohhhh, hi, Ricky. *(HE turns to Lynn.)* Listen, Ricky, let me call you back. I'll call you back from the car-phone, okay? I'll call you back ... That was Ricky.

JEFF. Who's Ricky?

LYNN. His mechanic.

TONY. I'm going to call him back from the car-phone.

LYNN. Why?

TONY. I just want him to listen to something. Back in a second. *(TONY exits.)*

JEFF. So, uh ... Tony has a car phone?

LYNN. Everyone here has a car phone. If you can't afford a car phone, you buy a fake plastic phone and drive around talking to yourself. Would you like a beer or something?

JEFF. A beer would be ... great.

(LYNN exits into the kitchen. The door swings closed behind her. JEFF talks towards her.)

JEFF. I just wish I ... wasn't so weird right now. *(Beat.)* I got a C minus on my Bankruptcy Law exam. It's

the first time I've gotten below an A in any of my courses.
I might have done even worse on my other exams. I can't
seem to concentrate. I read something, and two seconds
later I look up and say ... "What did I just read?" (*Beat.*) I
saw a TV show recently on this ... black civil rights
lawyer in the fifties, and he said ... a lawyer is either a
social engineer, or a leach on society. And I thought to
myself that's what I'm going to be. (*Beat.*) A leech. (*Beat.*)
It's like my life is ... deconstructing in front of my eyes,
and now I'm ... here, and the only thing I can think of is
... you, Lynn. From the moment that Tony called to invite
me, I've ... been thinking of you, and I ... Oh my God,
what am I doing, I can't believe I'm ... saying this aloud,
am I losing my mind? I'm sorry, I'm terribly sorry, this is
... unconscionable, I'm ... just going to leave. I'll fly back
to New York. Please forgive me.

(HE stands up. LYNN comes in from the kitchen, holding
two beers.)

   LYNN. Excuse me? Did you say something? I couldn't
hear in the kitchen.
   JEFF. Oh no, nothing ... So, uh ... how's it going?
   LYNN. Fine.
   JEFF. Fine? Great.
   LYNN. Well, actually, I'm not great. Just fine.
   JEFF. Oh, I'm sorry.
   LYNN. There's nothing to be sorry about. I'm fine.
   JEFF. Hunh ... (*JEFF shakes his head.*)
   LYNN. What?
   JEFF. I was just thinking about the first time I ever
saw you. Never mind. So, uh ... how's ... Tony?

LYNN. He's thrilled that you and Fred would come to L.A. for this.

JEFF. For what?

LYNN. For the People's Most Popular Awards.

JEFF. Oh yeah, well, you know. It's great that uh ... Tony's such a big success. But he was always very ... popular.

LYNN. Un-hunh.

JEFF. In high-school, he was popular. Fred was popular, but Tony was really ... popular.

LYNN. Hunh.

JEFF. I was never, you know ... popular.

LYNN. Popularity isn't everything.

JEFF. But you, I mean you ...

LYNN. What? I what?

JEFF. You were very ... very ... popular. I mean everybody, everybody, you know. Wanted to get to know you.

LYNN. Seriously?

JEFF. Oh sure. (*JEFF sighs.*)

LYNN. Are you alright?

JEFF. Oh sure, sure, I guess it's ... all that pot.

LYNN. You're stoned?

JEFF. No, I mean ... in high-school. We ... Tony, Fred and I ... smoked a lot of pot together. He probably told you.

LYNN. Only a few thousand times.

JEFF. We used to ... stand out there in the outfield, just ... incredibly stoned. Me in left field, Tony in ... center, and Fred in ... right. All three of us ... stoned off our asses. Maybe that's ... why we lost so many games.

(The PHONE rings.)

LYNN. Excuse me. ... Hello? ... Shit! *(SHE hangs up.)*
Someone keeps calling and hanging up.
JEFF. Maybe it's ... an obscene caller.
LYNN. They don't say anything. They just hang up.
JEFF. Then maybe it's ... not an obscene caller.
LYNN. Unless he's using sign language.
JEFF. *(Sips his beer painfully.)* So, uh ... how's
teaching?
LYNN. Teaching? It's going well.
JEFF. Yeah? You're ... enjoying it?
LYNN. Un-hunh ... It's a pretty boring subject.
JEFF. What subject are you teaching?
LYNN. I meant that teaching is sort of a boring
subject.
JEFF. Why?
LYNN. I don't know. I mean I don't find it boring, but
... it seems like other people do.
JEFF. Oh ... Why?
LYNN. Because they're shallow, insignificant assholes,
I guess. Whoops, did that sound bitter? I don't mean to be
bitter. Actually, term is over, I'm just in the middle of
writing comment cards.
JEFF. Really? I'd love to ... read them sometime.
LYNN. What, my third grade comment cards?
JEFF. Yes.
LYNN. Are you serious?
JEFF. Yes.

(TONY comes in through the front door.)

TONY. Sorry about that.

JEFF. I think I'll ... uh ...

TONY. Hey, Jeff! (*JEFF stops.*) Where you going?

JEFF. I'm just going to uh ... wash my hands. (*JEFF exits.*)

TONY. I hope Fred gets here soon.

LYNN. Well, I guess I'd better change.

TONY. Oh, yeah, sweetheart, I got you something. Close your eyes. (*HE takes out a box from his pocket.*)

LYNN. You got me something?

TONY. Yup.

LYNN. Thanks.

TONY. You don't know what it is yet. (*HE puts it in her hand.*)

LYNN. It's a box.

TONY. There's something inside it.

LYNN. The suspense is killing me. (*SHE opens the box.*) Wow, they're beautiful.

TONY. They're emeralds.

LYNN. Emeralds? Jesus, Tony.

TONY. Try them on.

(*LYNN puts on the emerald earrings. Goes over to a mirror.*)

LYNN. Tony, they're magnificent. They're real emeralds?

TONY. Unless I got ripped off. Yeah, they're real.

LYNN. God, they must cost a fortune. They must cost more than I make in a month.

TONY. They're not so expensive.

LYNN. And I can keep them? I mean they're not rented or anything?

TONY. No, they're not rented. What do you think I am? Some cheapskate?

LYNN. They're fantastic. (*SHE kisses him.*)

TONY. Listen, sweetie, umm ... I'm not sure what's ... what's been going on with us ... the last few months, but ...

LYNN. Tony ...

TONY. But, you know, I still ... I still ...

LYNN. Tony, please ...

TONY. I've got to be honest with you. You still really slaughter me. You're still ... the most beautiful girl I've ever laid eyes on.

LYNN. I'll never forget ... I'll never forget you standing there in the pouring rain, in a kimono, with a bottle of champagne in one hand, a bunch of orchids in the other.

TONY. I wanted to make an impression.

LYNN. "I'm in Dostoevsky class with you," you said. You were unshaven. You looked like you hadn't slept in a week.

TONY. I was hoping you'd take pity on me.

LYNN. I did. I let you in.

TONY. And look what happened.

LYNN. Yup.

(*TONY kisses her. SHE kisses him back. JEFF comes in.*)

JEFF. Oh ... excuse me.

LYNN. Jeff, look at these. Aren't they beautiful?

JEFF. Yeah, they're ... nice.

LYNN. What'll I wear them with?

TONY. Maybe that Chanel I just got you.

LYNN. I'll try it. (*LYNN exits up the stairs.*)

TONY. She's wonderful. Don't you think?

JEFF. What, about Lynn?

TONY. Isn't she's great?

JEFF. She's your girlfriend.

TONY. Of course she's my girlfriend. How's your room?

JEFF. Nice view of the pool.

TONY. Thanks for coming all the way to L.A, man, I really appreciate it.

JEFF. Thanks for inviting me.

TONY. Sure I can't pay for your ticket?

JEFF. No, that's alright—

TONY. —I wouldn't even be going to that stupid ceremony tomorrow—

JEFF. —I just got all that money—

TONY. —but my agent said I had to. So it'll be great having you and Fred there to laugh at the whole thing with me.

JEFF. It'll be good seeing Fred.

TONY. Yeah, the Three Musketeers together again. Or the Three Stooges or something.

JEFF. Congratulations about the uh ... nomination.

TONY. Thanks. My show's such a mindless crock of shit.

JEFF. Well, you know, it's a sit-com.

TONY. It's not even a sit-com. It's a shit-com. Have you seen it?

JEFF. What, "Model Detectives"? I've seen it ... a few times.

TONY. How could I write something like that? Two high-fashion models join the New York police department. What a crock.

JEFF. Well, good luck.

TONY. There's five shows nominated for best new series. I doubt I'll win.

JEFF. You'll probably win.

TONY. "Country Bumpkins" will probably win. It's even more brainless than my show. "Family Disasters" could win, but their ratings have been sliding. Then there's "Simple Miracles," that CBS show starring the guy without any arms and legs.

JEFF. I've heard of that.

TONY. But did you watch it?

JEFF. No.

TONY. You're not alone. The ad campaign they had: "*You will be moved,* for a half-hour, every Sunday at eight."

JEFF. Well, it's good they're ... focusing attention on disabled people.

TONY. Anything for a profit, which, unfortunately, they're not making, so it'll be off the air within the year. And there's "Homicidal Maniacs" on Fox, which really shouldn't be nominated, because it's a docu-drama, aside from reasons of good taste.

JEFF. That's the one where they reenact murders?

TONY. It's sort of a how-to show for kids.

JEFF. I don't know, I ... don't really watch much TV.

TONY. Of course not, because it's all such heinous, wretched bullshit. But what if we made shows you could enjoy even if you weren't the product of generations of inbreeding. What if we made the kind of shows that you and I would actually like to watch?

(Pause.)

JEFF. So, uh, how are your parents?

TONY. My parents? Well ... my mom's sleeping with some thirty-year-old copywriter at her office, and my dad ... who knows?

JEFF. You haven't talked to him?

TONY. Not in nine months. I flew ... I actually flew to Palm Beach to see him on my birthday—

JEFF. You flew there on your birthday?

TONY. Yeah, I must have been out of my mind. I went and surprised him at his house, we played a few rounds of golf, he got drunk off his ass, and I left the next morning. He never even realized it was my birthday.

JEFF. You didn't tell him?

TONY. Why give him the satisfaction? ... Who knows, though, maybe he'll call me tomorrow.

JEFF. Why?

TONY. You know, the awards. Maybe he'll call and wish me luck or something. So how have you been, man?

JEFF. Me? Uh ...

TONY. How's law school?

JEFF. Alright. Everyone there likes to argue. They all think they're so important because they're in law school.

TONY. Hunh. How's your mom?

JEFF. She's dead. She died ... four months ago. You wrote me a condolence letter.

TONY. ... Jeff, I'm sorry.

JEFF. That's alright.

TONY. What a stupid, self-involved prick I am.

JEFF. Don't be ... so hard on yourself.

TONY. I mean how could I ... how could I forget that?

JEFF. I don't know.

TONY. What does that say about me, that I'm capable of that? (*TONY sits down on the couch and stares at the carpet.*)

JEFF. Well, you know, man, it probably just slipped your mind. Could happen to anyone.

TONY. Anyone who's a complete asshole.

JEFF. Well, you've always been an asshole.

TONY. I have?

JEFF. Sure.

(*TONY springs up and hugs Jeff.*)

TONY. I'm so glad you're here!

(*The TWO OF THEM laugh.*)

TONY. Because I've been feeling like I'm ... losing touch with ... reality.

JEFF. Well, you know, what's reality? It's like ... my suitcase. I mean ... I spent so much time packing it, deciding what to wear, picking out the right socks to go with my slacks, and now ... it's in Europe, and it doesn't really matter.

TONY. But there is meaning. There's things like friendship, I mean that's intangible, but without it, human life would just sort of crumble into depravity, don't you think?

JEFF. Yeah ...

TONY. Listen, I was gonna wait until Fred got here to talk about this, but what the hell. Jeff, how'd you like to go into business with me?

JEFF. Business?

TONY. You, me and Fred. I've been thinking of forming a production company, and if I win this stupid People's Most Popular Award, I'll be in a great position to get it rolling. I need to work with people I trust, and you guys and Lynn are just about the only people who fit that description.

JEFF. What description?

TONY. I trust you. I thought you could be the legal person at the company, and Fred was always good at math—he could be the accountant and financial person. And you could both help me find material. Remember how we used to talk about books when we were in high school?

JEFF. We did?

TONY. That Russian Literature elective? Remember?

JEFF. Oh yeah, *War and Peace*.

TONY. And Chekhov.

JEFF. So you want to produce *War and Peace*?

TONY. Well ... just stuff we could be proud of. I even had some cards made up, just to see what it'd look like. Wanna see?

JEFF. (*Laughs.*) Sure.

(TONY takes out a card and hands it to Jeff.)

JEFF. "All For One Productions. Jeff Peters, Vice President for Legal Affairs."

TONY. If you don't like your title, you could change it.

JEFF. And uh, Fred would be the accountant, hunh?

TONY. Right. He'd be perfect, don't you think?

JEFF. Thought you told me he was into music now or something.

TONY. Yeah, but I don't know how serious he is about it.

(The DOORBELL rings. TONY opens the front door. JONNY LIGHTNINGROD is standing there. HE is dressed in a rumpled satin shirt and torn black jeans. His hair is cut unevenly. Spiky tufts stick out here and there. His skin is sallow.)

JONNY. Trick or treat!

TONY. ... Fred?

(JONNY claps Tony on the shoulder. The TWO OF THEM semi-embrace. JEFF comes over, smiling.)

JEFF. Hey.

JONNY. Fuck this handshake shit! *(JONNY hugs him.)*

JEFF. *(Laughs.)* Ow, you poked me in the eye with your hair.

JONNY. Jesus, Tony, is this your house? You're rich!

TONY. Fred, you look ... different!

JONNY. What, you mean the 'drobe?

TONY. "The drobe"?

JONNY. The wardrobe.

TONY. You look like the Tasmanian Devil.

JONNY. *(Looks around.)* Wow, Tony. You should see where I live. It's this one room apartment in the Tenderloin. There's like thirty Cambodian refugees in the apartment next door, I can hear them smacking their kids all day, the walls are paper thin. You guys wanna do some blow?

TONY. What, now?

JONNY. I thought I'd ask before my girlfriend comes in, because she's like a vacuum cleaner. (*JONNY goes over to the coffee table and pulls out a brown vial of coke.*) Jeff, want some blow?

JEFF. (*Laughs.*) No, not right now.

JONNY. It's good blow, man. I couldn't afford it, but I always sell half of what I score so it ends up not costing me anything. (*HE taps out some coke onto the table and screws the cap back on.*) I figure it's immoral to sell drugs if you make a profit, but if you're just using the money to buy your own drugs, that's okay. Tony, come on over here. (*JONNY takes out a razor blade and cuts a line.*)

TONY. Uh, gee, I wish I could, but I really don't do coke any more.

JONNY. Why not?

TONY. I'm just not around it much. People don't really do coke any more.

JONNY. What do they do?

TONY. Ginseng?

JONNY. Well would you like some heroin?

TONY. You have heroin too?

JONNY. Maybe, if you want some.

TONY. No, thanks.

JONNY. Jeff?

JEFF. No, that's alright.

JONNY. Okay, well, I don't have it anyway, so don't worry about it. Sure you guys don't want any blow? ... Fine, leaves more for me. (*JONNY leans down and snorts.*) El queso blanco. That's what they call me where I work.

JEFF. Where do you work?

JONNY. I'm a busboy at a Mexican restaurant. I also swab up after the dinner shift is through, so I'm sort of a janitor. Pretty fucking ironic. (*JONNY leans down and snorts another line.*) Every restaurant in America has illegal Mexicans doing the shitwork, and here I am, a college educated, Park Avenue white guy, swabbing up at night in a Mexican restaurant. (*JONNY rubs the leftover coke into his gums.*) Wow. Good blow. But look, man, don't get me wrong, my music is really getting going. In fact a guy who works for a record company came and saw my gig last week, and he was really positive, said he loved the tunes, I have copies of the album I made, they're in my girlfriend's backpack, things are really looking good.

TONY. You didn't tell me your girlfriend was coming up, Fred. In fact you didn't tell me you had a girlfriend.

JONNY. Yeah, well, she really wanted to come meet my two old buddies.

TONY. That's fine, glad to have her. I don't know if she can go tomorrow, though, to the awards ceremony, I only have a certain number of seats.

JONNY. That's alright, no big deal.

TONY. I'll try my best to get another one.

JONNY. No sweat, Tony. By the way, I have something I want to talk with you about. Sort of an idea I have.

TONY. Really? So do I—

JONNY (*Not listening.*) Maybe I'll tell you later. Now's not the time.

TONY. Okay.

JONNY. Sure you don't want any drugs of any kind?

TONY. No thanks, Fred, really.

JONNY. Listen, can I ask both you guys a favor? Please don't call me Fred. In November I had my name legally changed to Jonny Lightningrod, which is, of course, my stage name. So if you guys could call me Jonny, it would be much appreciated. Being called Fred just makes me feel, I don't know, it gives me the creeps, you know what I mean? Because I don't feel like a Fred any more. I don't even look like a Fred. Do I look like a Fred, Jeff?

JEFF. I guess not.

JONNY. You'll get used to it. So Jonny, or J.L. would be fine too. You don't have to call me "Mister Lightningrod," at least not until I have a platinum record. That was a joke. You guys can always call me Jonny. Or "El Queso Blanco," the White Cheese, whichever you prefer. I haven't sent either of you guys my album yet, have I?

TONY. No.

JEFF. No.

(JONNY opens the front door and yells.)

JONNY. HEY FARRAH! Album's in her backpack. HEY! HEY, FARRAH!

FARRAH. *(Off.)* What?!

JONNY. What are you doing out there?

(FARRAH comes in. SHE's carrying a huge hiker's backpack. SHE's seventeen. SHE wears a tie-dyed t-shirt and tight jeans.)

FARRAH. There's a Porsche out there.

JONNY. Guys, this is my girlfriend, Farrah. Farrah, these are my old, old friends from New York, we all went to high school and grade school together. This is Jeff.

FARRAH. Hi, is that your Porsche?

JEFF. No.

JONNY. And this is Tony.

FARRAH. It's your Porsche?

TONY. Sort of gauche, hunh?

FARRAH. Excuse me?

JONNY. I'm gonna get a record out of your pack.

FARRAH. Let me take it off my back first? (*FARRAH slings the heavy pack onto the floor.*)

JONNY. Careful!

FARRAH. Why? You have like thirteen hundred more.

JONNY. Not with me, I don't.

FARRAH. His whole closet is, like, stacked with records. Also, he's glued all these album covers to the walls. So it's like "Jonny Lightningrod" all over the place.

JONNY. So, I'm a megalomaniac. We all have our problems.

FARRAH. ... Wow, so this is it. L.A. Tinseltown. I've always wanted to come here, all my life, and now here I am, in the flesh, and all I can say is: *score!*

TONY. That about covers it. How was your drive?

FARRAH. The drive? Don't make me laugh. His Volkswagen Beetle has like a top speed of thirty miles an hour on the freeway. I thought we were gonna be road kill for some eighteen-wheeler.

JONNY. You took all that shit along. It weighed the car down. Tony, this is for you. And Jeff, this is for you.

(HE hands each of them an album. On the cover is a picture of Jonny, with JONNY LIGHTNINGROD printed above it.)

JEFF. *(Reads.)* "Jonny Lightningrod."

JONNY. That's me, man. That's my album.

TONY. So, you're ... really pursuing music, hunh?

JONNY. Music is my life, Tony. Of course it's not just music, it's the image, too.

TONY. I can see that.

(JEFF looks at the back of the album.)

JEFF. *(Reads.)* "All songs written and performed by Jonny Lightningrod. All songs produced by Jonny Lightningrod. Copyright, 1995, Lightningrod Music."

FARRAH. Can you believe he made fifteen hundred of those things?

JONNY. Fifteen hundred is nothing.

FARRAH. Think of all the drugs you could have bought.

TONY. Thanks for the album.

JONNY. Wanna hear it? Where's your record player?

TONY. I don't have a record player. Only compact disc.

JONNY. Compact disc? *(JONNY stops dead.)* You mean you don't have a record player in this whole house?

TONY. No.

JONNY. Where do you play your records?

TONY. I don't have any records. ... Sorry.

JONNY. *(Quietly.)* That's alright, Tony. Everything's compact disc nowadays. The whole world's going to shit.

FARRAH. So, Tony, how did you get all this money?

TONY. I'm the head writer for a TV sitcom.

FARRAH. No way.

TONY. Yeah. Believe it or not, they actually have writers.

FARRAH. Which sitcom?

TONY. I'm sort of embarrassed to say.

FARRAH. You're fucking with me. You don't really write TV. (*SHE turns to Jeff.*) He's pulling my leg, isn't he?

JEFF. Uh, no.

FARRAH. Which show? Which show do you write?

TONY. "Model Detectives." But please don't blame me.

FARRAH. "Model Detectives"? You write "*Model Detectives*"?

TONY. It writes itself, really.

FARRAH. I *love* "Model Detectives"! It's my favorite show.

TONY. Oh. I'm sorry.

FARRAH. Blow my mind. In my opinion, Model Detectives is the best thing on TV since Charlie's Angels. And you know why? Because it's beautiful women with guns. It's like, okay, you have these two babes up there: there's Cindy Davis, the blonde Sex Kitten, and Alexis Thomson, the brunette Ice Goddess. They're both super vixens, but the thing is, they have guns, and nobody can fuck with them. Am I right?

TONY. I just hope they don't own guns in real life.

FARRAH. I have only one bone to pick with you.

TONY. What's that?

FARRAH. You should go easier on the comedy, and make it a bit more serious, like "Charlie's Angels" was.

JONNY. I knew I should have brought my guitar. If I had my guitar I could just play the songs for you, I'm sure you'd dig them, the lyrics are really sarcastic for the most part, maybe I'll sing them for you later.

TONY. So, are you still ... interested in math at all?

(LYNN comes down the stairs.)

LYNN. Hi!
JONNY. Lynn! Man, it's been a long time.

(LYNN and JONNY hug.)

JONNY. You look beautiful as always.
FARRAH. Fuck you, Jonny.
JONNY. What?
FARRAH. Nothing. I just think it's impolite to compliment one woman without complimenting the other woman who's standing right there in the same room.
JONNY. What? You look beautiful too.
FARRAH. Too late now. *(FARRAH smiles and holds her hand out to Lynn.)* My name's Farrah. Like Farrah Fawcett.
LYNN. Nice to meet you.
TONY. Farrah's our surprise guest star.
FARRAH. I drove down with Jonny.
LYNN. I'm Lynn.
FARRAH. Great to meet you, Lynn. And what's your connection here?
LYNN. I live here.
FARRAH. Wow. Nice house.
LYNN. Thanks. Has Tony showed you your room yet?

TONY. No, I haven't. Hope you guys don't mind there's only one bed. It's big, though.

JONNY. Why should we mind?

TONY. We'd better get rolling, there's a party I sort of have to go to.

FARRAH. What, like a Hollywood party? Awesome.

LYNN. Your room's down this way.

(FARRAH picks up her backpack.)

FARRAH. I have a couple of suitcases out in the car, but I can get them later.

TONY. *(Laughs.)* What are you, moving in?

FARRAH. Can I?

TONY. *(Laughs.)* No.

(LYNN and FARRAH exit into the hall.)

FARRAH. *(Off.)* Are there gonna be any stars at this party?

JONNY. Uh, Tony ...

(TONY pauses at the entrance.)

JONNY. Never mind. I'll talk to you later.

TONY. Don't you want to see your room?

JONNY. No, that's alright.

(TONY exits into the hall.)

JEFF. How old is your girlfriend?

JONNY. Seventeen.

JEFF. That's not illegal, is it?

JONNY. I don't know.

JEFF. How old are you now? Twenty-six?

JONNY. Yeah.

JEFF. Me too. Almost twenty-seven. ... Never thought I'd be this old.

JONNY. You're telling me. Whose beers are these?

JEFF. One of them's mine, one of them's Lynn's.

JONNY. Mind if I finish them? I have to mellow out here a little.

JEFF. There's more beer in the fridge.

JONNY. That's alright. I don't like 'em too cold, gives me a headache.

JEFF. So, are you ... doing a lot of cocaine?

JONNY. Who, me? No, you know, a little every now and then.

JEFF. And heroin?

JONNY. Heroin? Who said heroin?

JEFF. You did earlier.

JONNY. You know, every now and then, maybe I do a little smack. (*JONNY moves on to the second beer.*) Anyway, it's good to see you, man.

JEFF. You too.

JONNY. You look ... older.

JEFF. So do you.

JONNY. I do? Shit. (*JONNY belches.*) Excuse me. ... Look, man, maybe this is totally tactless, but I'm sorry about your mother.

JEFF. Thanks.

JONNY. She was very cool. She was always a very cool woman.

JEFF. ... Yeah ...

JONNY. Remember that time she took us all to the Bob Dylan concert? We were like, "Who the fuck is Bob Dylan?"

JEFF. She xeroxed the lyrics to the songs and handed them out to us before the concert.

JONNY. I was afraid she was gonna quiz us.

JEFF. She did! She made us talk about what the songs meant, don't you remember?

JONNY. Oh yeah, that's right. Wow, that was a long time ago. Anyway, I was really sad to hear about it.

JEFF. Thanks. Uh ... how are your parents?

JONNY. They're still wearing Polo. So how you doing? You doing alright? What's that law school shit like?

JEFF. I try not to think about it. I just try and get through it, at this point. I have one more year.

JONNY. Then what?

JEFF. Then I guess I go to some law firm and work seventy hours a week.

JONNY. You could always drop out.

JEFF. (*Laughs.*) Yeah, my mother would love that. (*JEFF freezes.*) Jesus.

JONNY. ... What? Are you alright?

JEFF. ... Yeah ... I just ... What I just said ... I'm twisted.

JONNY. Join the club.

(*TONY comes in from the hall.*)

TONY. Hey, guys! Having a good time yet?
JONNY. Sure.
JEFF. Un-hunh.

TONY. Thanks so much for coming to L.A. It means a lot to me. It's basically impossible to have friends out here, because everyone you meet is desperate. They're all desperate to get something from you, or sell you something, or prove they're more important then you. Every party I go to is an obstacle course, it's always business. To be honest with you, I sort of forgot I had friends. After a while, you begin to think that's all there is, you know, operating. That's all there is to human relationships. Everyone's an operator.

(LYNN and FARRAH enter from the hall.)

FARRAH. This is just what I imagined L.A. would be like.

LYNN. Un-hunh.

FARRAH. I *love* that fucking marble tub.

LYNN. I'm glad.

FARRAH. Hey, Jonny, why don't you break out some blow?

JONNY. Not right now, Farrah.

FARRAH. Why not?

JONNY. No one wants to do any.

FARRAH. What do you mean?

JONNY. I already asked these guys, and they don't want to do any.

FARRAH. Oh. Nobody wants to do it, hunh? *(Beat.)* Okay, forget it.

LYNN. I'll do some.

TONY. You will?

LYNN. Yeah.

TONY. Why?

LYNN. Why not?
JONNY. Well, come on over here.

(JONNY taps some coke out onto the table and hands Lynn a pre-rolled dollar bill. LYNN leans down and snorts.)

LYNN. Thanks.

(TONY is watching her.)

TONY. Are you happy with yourself?
LYNN. Yes.
TONY. Well, uh ... we'd better get going to this party, guys, if you could ... put away the drugs for a minute.
JONNY. Sure, sure, Tony.
JEFF. *(To Lynn.)* That's a ... nice dress.
LYNN. Thanks.
FARRAH. Okay, let's go, party time!

(TONY opens the door for everyone. HE puts his hand on Jonny's shoulder.)

TONY. Hey, I dug up my old Strat-o-matic Baseball game.
JONNY. Oh, uh, you did?
TONY. Maybe we can play when we get back. And do some talking.
JONNY. Sure, sure, no problem.
TONY. But this time, you're not getting Lou Gehrig!
JONNY. Hah-hah, right ...

(JONNY exits, followed by JEFF, LYNN and FARRAH. TONY is almost out the door when the PHONE rings. HE hurries back in, thinks about picking it up, then decides against it and leaves. BLACKOUT.)

Scene 2

NIGHT. A few hours after the end of scene one. TONY is sitting alone at the table, hunched over his Strat-o-matic Baseball game. His shirt is untucked, his jacket is draped over a chair. It's after the party. HE is full of energy, doing play-by-play commentary for himself.

TONY. Nineteen sixty-five Sandy Koufax pitching to nineteen forty-one Joe DiMaggio, what a confrontation, Ty Cobb's on second, taking a big lead, trying to rattle Koufax, but the intense lefty is concentrating on home plate, DiMaggio steps in, he's been on a tear lately, Koufax winds up, he's perhaps the most valuable pitcher in the all-star Strat-o-matic league, he won't pitch on Saturdays because of his religious beliefs, it's Jew against Catholic with Ty Cobb on second, the game tied at one-one. The pitch— *(TONY shakes the dice and rolls them on the game board.)* It's a one–nine, Oh my God, single one to six, lineout seven to twenty! *(TONY picks an orange card.)* Four! It's a single, a blooper over the diving first baseman's outstretched mitt! DiMaggio is safe at first and Cobb pulls in to third! Boy, when you're on a hot streak, it seems like all the balls fall for you!

(FARRAH comes in.)

FARRAH. What are you, talking to yourself?

TONY. I talk to myself all the time. And let me tell you, I bore the shit out of me.

FARRAH. That party was great! *Both* the stars were there. I never thought I'd actually get to meet Cindy Davis and Alexis Thomson. But I guess you see them every day.

TONY. Not if I'm lucky.

FARRAH. Are you nervous about the awards tomorrow?

TONY. Nervous?

FARRAH. If I were you, I'd be climbing the walls. I mean the People's Most Popular Award, do you know how important that is? All of America votes for it. It's not like the Academy Award or the Nobel Prize, where you don't know *who* the fuck chose the winner. With the People's Most Popular Award, everyone gets to vote. It's right there in the *TV Guide.*

TONY. Did you vote?

FARRAH. Of course I voted.

TONY. ... Did you vote for "Model Detectives" for best new series?

FARRAH. Fuckin' A.

TONY. Does that mean you did or you didn't?

FARRAH. It means I did. (*SHE leans over Tony's shoulder.*) What on earth are you doing?

TONY. Mickey Cochrane is up with two outs and men on first and third.

FARRAH. Oh. Well that makes sense.

TONY. (*Rolls the dice.*) The pitch—shit! Shit!

FARRAH. What?

TONY. Groundball to the shortstop. Inning's over. Man, that Koufax is some pitcher.

FARRAH. I don't know *what* you're talking about.

TONY. Okay. Bottom of the seventh. Hoyt Wilhelm on the mound.

FARRAH. Do you think you could stop that for a minute? I'm trying to have a conversation with you.

TONY. Sorry. Got a little excited there.

FARRAH. By who?

TONY. By Sandy Koufax. Where is everyone?

FARRAH. Out at the pool. Jonny lit up a joint, but nobody wanted any.

TONY. So is he pretty ... stoned ... most of the time?

FARRAH. You could say that, I guess. (*FARRAH sits down and props her legs up on the table.*) Man, that was embarrassing when he started handing out his album at the party. He'd give his record to anyone. If he got to meet, like, Mother Theresa, he'd hand her his album. You know his parents are rich?

TONY. I've known him since we were ten.

FARRAH. Why does he want to live in the Tenderloin? That neighborhood is fucked. It's where the transvestite whores hang out, there's some nasty leather bars there, and Cambodian gangs, there's always some drug dealer rubbing out another drug dealer. Not that I haven't been around, I've been around, but ... his parents are rich! It doesn't matter, none of my business.

TONY. Well, it's good that you care about him.

FARRAH. I didn't say I care about him, I just said I don't understand why, if he's got rich parents ... I mean he's a good guy and everything, he's pretty cool, he's crazy. That first night I met him, that was crazy, but to be honest with you ...

TONY. ... What? ...

FARRAH. You're more my type.

(Silence. TONY takes a deep breath and exhales it audibly. HE stands up.)

FARRAH. What? What's wrong?

TONY. "What's wrong?" For the first thing, you're Fred's girlfriend.

FARRAH. Who's Fred?

TONY. I mean Jonny. You're Jonny's girlfriend.

FARRAH. Who told you I was his girlfriend?

TONY. Aren't you?

FARRAH. I met him three weeks ago at a bar. I mean yeah, we had some sex, but calling me his girlfriend is like an exaggeration.

TONY. Terrific.

FARRAH. And just so you know, I completely use protection. I have these nasty black condoms that are made for guys to have anal sex, they're called Tractor condoms, they could stop a bullet.

TONY. Un-hunh. And for a second thing, despite the fact that you are vaguely attractive in some Lolita-like way, I've been trying very hard not to sleep around.

FARRAH. Why?

TONY. Because I'm living with someone. I'm living with Lynn, in case you hadn't noticed.

FARRAH. Yeah, but you two aren't right for each other.

TONY. We've been together for four years.

FARRAH. It's like oil and water. You don't mix.

TONY. I guess I'm supposed to be the oil.

FARRAH. You got it. Anyway, I'm probably ... a little out of line here, but I had a few drinks at the party, and I always call 'em like I see 'em.

TONY. Listen, sweetheart, not all honesty is refreshing.

FARRAH. I'm just saying that possibly you might want to try someone like me, who has completely unlimited potential.

TONY. For what?

FARRAH. For anything. The world is my oyster. In a few hours I might feel like shooting myself in the head, in fact, I probably will. But right now, sitting here with you, I have this feeling that life can be whatever we want. Anything we imagine, we can make it come true.

TONY. I think that's called manic depression.

FARRAH. Call it what you like. I just have, you know, the killer instinct. I generally get what I want. You don't even know the half of it.

TONY. Right, well, it's been interesting talking with you, Farrah. I wish you lots of success in your future endeavors.

FARRAH. Hey, I was just being honest about my take on the situation here. I didn't mean to disturb your baseball game.

(The kitchen door opens and LYNN comes in.)

TONY. Lynn!

LYNN. What?

TONY. Hi, honey.

FARRAH. Think I'll go unpack a few of my things. Lynn, are you going for a swim later?

LYNN. I don't think so.

(FARRAH exits.)

TONY. That girl is like the Exorcist Part Four.

LYNN. Why do you say that?

TONY. Fred really knows how to pick 'em. He used to have this girlfriend, Claudia, we nicknamed her "the fish," because—

LYNN. I know.

TONY. Because she—

LYNN. I know why you nicknamed her "the fish." I don't need to hear it again.

TONY. Uh ... okay. Boy, I'm really ... wondering whether Fred would make such a good accountant anymore.

LYNN. You're wondering if he'd be a good accountant?

TONY. I'd have to, like, urine test him.

LYNN. What makes you think Fred would want to be an accountant?

TONY. Not just an accountant. V.P. in charge of business affairs. It's better than being a busboy.

LYNN. I'd be surprised if Fred has much short term memory left. I don't think you should trust him with your finances.

TONY. Really?

LYNN. Yeah, really. What are you, an idiot?

TONY. Uh ... is that a rhetorical question?

(LYNN fixes herself a drink.)

LYNN. Tony, can I ask you something?

TONY. Sure.

LYNN. I heard something at the party. Someone told me something. A rumor.

TONY. "A rumor"?

LYNN. Someone told me that everyone thinks you're sleeping with one of the actresses on the show. They're just not sure which one.

TONY. What?

LYNN. That's what someone told me.

TONY. Someone? Who is someone? I'll break their neck!

LYNN. You don't have to get all excited.

TONY. I don't? (*TONY starts pacing around in a circle.*) Who told you this? Who?

LYNN. No one. It doesn't matter who.

TONY. Was it that—You were talking to fucking Mike Gonzalez for a long time at the party.

LYNN. What makes you think it was Mike?

TONY. Because he's the hairdresser, that's what! Don't you know hairdressers are addicted to gossip? The more of a lie it is, the better! Mike can't help himself! He's notorious!

LYNN. (*Calmly.*) So you're saying it's not true?

TONY. That fucking—it was Mike Gonzalez, wasn't it? I'll have his ass fired from the show.

LYNN. Tony, please try not to be repulsive.

TONY. ... Repulsive? ... You think I'm repulsive?

LYNN. ... Tony, is it true or not? Are you sleeping with one of the actresses on the show?

TONY. No. No, I'm not sleeping with anyone. I love you. I love you, Lynn.

LYNN. ... I don't know, Tony, it's just ... here I am.. I mean look at me, I'm in this house, which you bought with your money, I'm living here. I'm ... what am I? I'm a teacher. I teach third grade. ... Have you even noticed that I teach third grade? I'm writing my report cards now.

TONY. I know that. What do you mean? I know you teach third grade.

LYNN. Please, let me talk. (*Beat.*) It's just that you ... you have a right, Tony. You have a right to whatever you want. And I really don't want to ask anything of you. It's exciting, what you're going through. I'm proud of you. I'm ... It's wonderful, the show, and ... money, but ...

(*The kitchen door opens and JONNY and JEFF come in. JONNY has a bottle of Jack Daniels in his hand.*)

JONNY. (*Sings.*) Hoo-ray for Hollywood! Hoo-ray, hoo-ray, hoo-ray for Hollywood! Let's take our pants off and dance in the nude, 'cause it's Hollywood, da, da, da.

JEFF. Did you make that up just now?

JONNY. Amazing how fast my mind works, hunh? Hey, it's Big Tony, alright! You missed the joint. Know what we need? Some Colt 45. Remember how we used to drink Colt 45 during practise? There was that patch of tall grass in centerfield, we'd hide the cans out there and take slugs off 'em between innings. Yes, sir, tho-o-o-se— were—the—days, my friend, (*HE sings.*) I thought they'd never end, those were the days, the motherfuckin' days!

LYNN. Think I might call it a night.

JONNY. I'm sorry, I was being loud.

LYNN. Be as loud as you want, I'm just tired.

TONY. Are you alright?

LYNN. Sure, I'm fine. Excuse me, guys, I'm sorry to be a drag.

JEFF. You're not a drag.

LYNN. Thanks. Goodnight.

TONY. Wait, I'll ... come up with you.

LYNN. No, I'm alright, I'm just gonna write some report cards and hit the sack. (*SHE exits up the stairs.*)

JONNY. So, Big Tony, tomorrow's the day!

TONY. "Big Tony"? Why are you calling me "Big Tony"?

JONNY. I don't know, for a moment you looked like a mafia don. Would you guys like me to sing a few of my songs? I almost brought my guitar, but Farrah put so much crap in the car. Wanna hear a song called "Dead Heartbeats"? It's the first song on side B of my album. There's also some political songs, there's "I ran from Iran, but I rock in Iraq!" Along more direct lines, there's "Fuk Tipper Gore." That's spelled F-U-K by the way. See I'm basically doing hardcore, but as a solo artist.

TONY. Umm, Fred—Jonny, ...

JONNY. It's just I want you to hear them, because I have a proposition to make to you.   (*JONNY takes a swig of Jack Daniels.*)

TONY. A proposition?

JONNY. Un-hunh.

TONY. That's funny, because I had sort of a proposition too.

JEFF. Would you like me to leave?

JONNY. No, don't leave, we're all friends.

JEFF. Yeah, but if you wanna talk something over with Tony—

JONNY. Okay, Tony, here it is. Should I just tell you?

TONY. Sure. And then I'll tell you mine.

JONNY. Maybe I'll sit down. Jeff, you wanna sit down too?

JEFF. Uh ...

JONNY. Sit down, man, it's making me nervous you standing up. Alright. Alright. Tony, ...

TONY. ... Yes? ...

JONNY. I have a proposition for you. (*Beat.*) Okay, like, I've watched your show, "Model Detectives," I rented a TV for a night and watched.

TONY. You rented a TV?

JONNY. Yeah, you can do that. Anyway, I rented a TV and watched ... most of the show. And watching it, I had an idea.

TONY. ... to turn it off?

JONNY. The idea was, how about an episode where the two model detectives go into a bar, and there's this guy playing at the bar, a solo hardcore musician, and one of the models falls in love with him. Or maybe they both fall in love with him, I don't know how kinky you wanna get.

(*HE looks for Tony's reaction. TONY has none.*)

JONNY. That was a joke, I mean I think it's much better if only one of them falls in love with him. So I was thinking, you know, that I would be good for the role of the musician. I figure you could show me in concert, you know, just a few songs, then they walk into the bar, and it's like, bang, who is this guy, this Jonny Lightningrod? (*Beat.*) I mean of course none of this makes sense because you haven't seen me play yet, so you don't know if I'm good or not. What do you think, Tone?

TONY. Uh ...

JONNY. You can be completely honest with me.

TONY. So you mean ... you want to be on the show.

JONNY. Exactly. (*Beat.*) Look, I'm not expecting an immediate yes or no on this, I just thought I'd run the idea by you and get some feedback. I just thought it would be an interesting plot twist for your show, and it would give me some much needed exposure. What do *you* think, Jeff?

JEFF. Uh, I'm really not ... I don't watch that much T.V.

JONNY. Tony? Just give me your first reaction, whatever's on your mind.

TONY. So the idea is that one of the Model Detectives falls in love with you. And then I suppose we write you in as a regular character.

JONNY. Hey, that would be great.

TONY. ... Maybe I should run my idea by you.

JONNY. Okay, so say I'm only in one episode, say it's just the one.

TONY. There are sponsors, Jonny.

JONNY. So what, I can sell Hondas. You don't think I can sell Hondas?

TONY. Well, I'll ... I'll think about it.

JONNY. Alright, say they don't fall in love with me. No one falls in love with me. They just come into this bar, they have a scene in this bar, and I happen to be there, playing, maybe you could show a flyer with Jonny Lightningrod. How about that?

TONY. Maybe down the line there'll be an episode where they go into a bar. But they don't drink. The Model Detectives don't drink.

JONNY. They can order tonic water.

(JONNY looks to Jeff for support. JEFF inches back slightly.)

JONNY. Alright, you said down the line, like when do you think? Within a month? Two months?

TONY. Why are you putting this pressure on me?

JONNY. I'm just asking to be a fucking extra, man, I just need a little exposure.

TONY. It's not that simple.

JONNY. Just have them go into a bar!

TONY. Look, I'll try, alright? But I don't really have the power to just do whatever I want with the show. We're under strict control, we're controlled by the network people who make the real decisions.

JONNY. Oh, bullshit, I saw you at the party tonight, everyone was sucking your ass, people were like, oh, are you a friend of Tony's?

TONY. Can I ask you one question? What the hell happened to math? You were a math whiz, for Christ's sake!

JONNY. That was a million years ago!

TONY. No it wasn't. It was ... what? Five years ago.

JONNY. Tony, look. Basically I don't give two fucks, it was just an idea which I thought might liven up your show a little. So don't do me any favors. I'm gonna fuckin' make it. Last gig I had, this dude comes up to me afterwards and says, "Hey I really dig your songs." And the guy hands me a card and it turns out he works for a record company, so I happen to have one of my albums there, and I give it to him, and he says, "Great, we're always looking for new talent." (*JONNY drinks.*) "We're always looking for new talent."

TONY. Well that's ... that's great.

JONNY. I'm gonna show you something. (*JONNY picks up his album, which was lying on the bar.*) Have you read this?

TONY. The album cover?

JONNY. Yes. The album cover. Listen to this. "When we look back on the history of rock and roll music, we will be able to see a clear division—before Jonny Lightningrod, and after Jonny Lightningrod. Jonny Lightningrod's cool guitar licks and driving vocals cannot mask the fact that he is at heart that rarest of things, a true rock original." Now if you'll excuse me, I'm gonna go see what my girlfriend is up to. (*HE exits into the hall.*)

TONY. Wait, wait, Fred—

(*JONNY's gone.*)

TONY. Well, looks like I didn't have to make up those business cards for Fred.

JEFF. I guess not.

TONY. He doesn't realize, the only thing the show could do is make fun of him. That's how it works. We give people what they want. We show life as they want to see it. And they don't want to see anything different. If it's different, we make fun of it.

JEFF. Is that ... in your contract?

TONY. Yeah, it's the famous "uphold mediocrity" clause.

JEFF. You know, he's just ... he's probably just struggling to make it. You know how that is.

TONY. Oh sure, well ... not really.

JEFF. You've never struggled? Well ... how about ... you know, other than work. You must have struggled somehow. Haven't you ever felt ... pain and fear so deep that your body seemed like ... an instrument being played by something greater than you are?

TONY. ... Guess I have something to look forward to. Well, at least *you're* not after anything from me.

(JEFF shifts uncomfortably in his seat.)

TONY. So what happened at the party? We were looking for you.

JEFF. Yeah I ... went for a walk.

TONY. That's a new one. Going for a walk in Bel Air. You're lucky you didn't get picked up by the police.

JEFF. I just felt like ... thinking.

TONY. So listen, man, even if ... even if Fred doesn't want to be a part of it..

JEFF. Tony, can I ask you a question?

TONY. I still think it would be a great thing if we could form a company together. And then when Fred sobers up ...

JEFF. How do you do it?

TONY. ... Do what?

JEFF. I don't know. Deal. You always seem to deal so well. You were always so sure of yourself. I can't imagine what that's like. I wish I was sure of myself. Sometimes I can't even ... decide whether to shave or have my cereal first. I sit there trying to decide. And when I try to think about the big decisions in life, it's totally hopeless.

TONY. Shave first, then have the cereal.

(The PHONE rings.)

TONY. I'll get it. ... Hello? Hi. Hi there. I can't talk now. I can't talk now. Do you speak English? I said I can't talk now. Bye-bye. *(TONY hangs up.)*

JEFF. Who was that?

TONY. No one, uh ... Cindy Davis. She's uh ... one of the Model Detectives, she just called 'cause she's up for best new actress tomorrow and she's nervous.

(The PHONE rings again. TONY jumps.)

TONY. I'll get it! ... Hello? I didn't hang up on you. I didn't. Please don't do that. Please don't do that. I'll talk with you tomorrow, not now. Don't call back. I'm sorry, but just don't call back. *(HE hangs up.)* Oh man, oh man, oh man.

JEFF. What?

TONY. Nothing. *(TONY paces in a circle.)* Oh man, oh man, oh man. Can I ask you something? I don't know if I should. I shouldn't. But I don't have anyone to talk to. Know what I mean?

JEFF. Yes.

TONY. Oh, man. Alright. Look, this is ... this is going to seem disgusting. I can't believe this myself, but ... I did something. I ... I slept with another woman.

JEFF. Who?

TONY. I slept with Cindy Davis. And I slept with Alexis Thomson. I slept with both of the actresses on my show.

JEFF. Wow. Those women are ... pretty attractive.

TONY. Every guy in America fantasizes about sleeping with these two bitches, and there they were throwing themselves at me.

JEFF. The blonde ... and the brunette?

TONY. It's hair dye.

JEFF. Really?

TONY. Believe me, I know. Anyway, the thing is, Alexis and Cindy hate each other. They can't stand each other. Cindy edged Alexis out for Hottest New Bombshell in an "Entertainment Weekly" poll, and it's been like a minefield on the set ever since. So now they ... they're both blackmailing me. They keep calling me at home, and I have to pretend it's my agent or my mechanic so I can take the call out in the car. Each one is threatening to tell Lynn if I don't fire the other one from the show!

JEFF. Does Lynn know?

TONY. No, she suspects, she suspects, but ... if she found out, my life would be over.

JEFF. Hunh. I mean, don't you uh ... respect Lynn?

TONY. Yeah, I respect her. I respect her more than I respect myself. What the hell's wrong with me? What should I do, Jeff?

JEFF. ... You're asking me?

TONY. Who else am I gonna ask?

JEFF. I don't know if I'm the best guy to ask ...

TONY. You're my oldest friend. I mean I need some advice here. Please.

JEFF. Well ... maybe you should tell her.

TONY. Tell her? Oh shit, oh Christ. ... Tell her?

(Jeff shrugs.)

TONY. I'd rather geld myself with a hot poker. (*Beat.*) But ... to be honest with you ... Lynn and I haven't ... we haven't really ... uh ...

JEFF. What?

TONY. Well, umm ... I'm sure it's just a temporary thing, you know, relationships have phases and everything. But uh ...

JEFF. But what?

TONY. ... For a while, we haven't been sleeping together. I guess she's ... going through some sort of phase where ... uh ...

(JONNY comes back in from the hall.)

TONY. Jonny! Great, you're back! Listen, man, I'm sorry, I'll definitely see what I can do in terms of getting you on the show, it'll probably just be extra work, but maybe we could get a flyer with your name on it in there, maybe I could do that, I'll try.

JONNY. Got a little surprise just now. I go into the bedroom, Farrah's lying in bed, reading a star map, and she's set up this boundary in the middle of the bed. She put pillows and stuff right down the middle of the bed. She's on one side, and I'm supposed to sleep on the other. I ask her what the fuck is up, but she won't talk to me, says she's busy reading. So I figure either she's turning Hassidic, or I'm getting dumped.

TONY. Shit.

JEFF. Sorry, man.

TONY. Maybe it's for the best.

JONNY. I feel old. That's the kind of thing *I* would have done when I was seventeen. Guess I was a stupid asshole for letting myself get the least bit attached in the first place. After all, I just met her three weeks ago, she's in San Francisco, she didn't even have a place to stay, but she had all this shit in a locker at the bus station. Expensive shit, like a compact disc player, eight pairs of Italian shoes. (*JONNY sits down.*) I don't know, are you guys able to have stable relationships? Because I'm not. The tops for me is a month. For about a month, I can make myself seem interesting, but then they find out what I'm really like, and that's that.

JEFF. Wow, what a coincidence.

JONNY. What?

JEFF. Well ... Tony was just telling me that uh ... Lynn and him aren't sleeping together anymore.

JONNY. Oh, wow, really?

TONY. (*Looks at Jeff.*) Uh, yeah. I didn't know there was gonna be a panel discussion about it.

JONNY. What's the deal, are you like ... not attracted to her anymore?

TONY. Me? ... No, no, I'm ... attracted. I'm still ... (*HE takes a breath.*) Pretty hot for her.

JONNY. Then she ...

JEFF. You mean she ...

TONY. She what?

JEFF. She doesn't ...

JONNY. She ain't into it?

TONY. ... Not really. I guess she ... temporarily ... (*TONY glances up the stairs.*) Is not into it, no.

JONNY. Ouch.

JEFF. No kidding.

JONNY. You guys have been together so long.

JEFF. Not at all, hunh?

JONNY. So we're batting 0 for 2 here.

TONY. Maybe it wasn't such a good idea for us to go to an all-boys school.

JONNY. How about you, Jeff?

JEFF. How about me what?

TONY. Yeah, how about you and the fairer sex?

JONNY. Are you banging anybody?

JEFF. Well, uh .... I can't say I've had that much ... experience ... with women.

JONNY. Are you gay?

JEFF. Uh ... no. I don't think so. I guess I've just been ... working too hard. But if I were ... lucky enough to ... meet someone, I'd probably say the most important thing would be ... that the two people be ... centered in themselves, and they ... hold each other ... sacred.

TONY. That's sort of beautiful, Jeff.

JONNY. Yeah ... (*Beat.*) Think I'll go shoot myself in the head. (*Beat.*) Wouldn't it be cool if President Clinton shot himself in the head? (*Beat.*) I mean like his friend shot himself. And that was neat. But wouldn't it be wild if President Clinton offed himself on national TV? If he just came on in a press conference and said like, "This country has too many problems, there's just nothing I can do about it," and then he blew his brains out in front of a hundred million viewers?

TONY. Fred, are you ... seeing a therapist by any chance?

JONNY. Hell no.

TONY. Maybe you should think about seeing one.

JONNY. I was in therapy from age five to age twelve. Seven years. Most people had babysitters. I had Doctor Nancy.

TONY. I asked my mom if I could see a shrink once, when I was fourteen. She said okay, and then she forgot.

JEFF. My dad was a shrink.

(TONY and FRED look at him.)

JEFF. That's all.

JONNY. You can't trust them.

TONY. Shrinks?

JONNY. Women.

TONY. You can trust some of them.

JONNY. No. None of them.

JEFF. How about your mother?

JONNY. No. Not even your mother.

TONY. Do you really believe that, or are you saying it for effect?

JONNY. For effect, I guess.

JEFF. But they are ... different.

TONY. They smell better.

JONNY. Some of them.

TONY. This is great. We're having an utterly moronic conversation.

JONNY. Yeah. How about that.

TONY. It's been a while since I've had a conversation like this.

JEFF. It's been a while since I had any sort of conversation at all.

(JONNY starts singing.)

JONNY. Ooh, Fa-arrah, Oh – oh – Fa-arrah, You spat on my heart, and then you tore it apart, You kicked both my balls, until I could barely crawl ... Oh – oh – Fa-arrah ...

TONY. Maybe you could be on my show.

JONNY. Really?

TONY. But wouldn't you rather have a more stable, yet more challenging life? Wouldn't you rather, for instance, be in charge of the finances for an up and coming production company?

JONNY. Why the hell would I want to do that?

TONY. Well what if Jeff and I were also running the company? What if it was the three of us working together, putting out kickass shows, and making an outrageous amount of money?

JONNY. But I wanna be a star.

TONY. Why? So you can have people worshipping some image of you that isn't even connected to what you're actually like as a person?

JONNY. Yeah, basically.

TONY. But you got a seven-ninety on your Math achievement tests.

JONNY. Should I say it real slow? "I'm ... a ... musician."

TONY. Okay. Sorry. I just ... want you guys to stick around a while. (*Beat.*) Anyone want to play Strat-o-matic Baseball?

JONNY. Jesus Christ, does this guy have a one-track mind, or what?

(JEFF laughs.)

JONNY. Alright, should we play this fuckin' game with him?

JEFF. Yeah, might as well. Or else he won't let us leave.

TONY. So you'll play? Great, let's pick teams.

JONNY. I get Lou Gehrig.

JEFF. I get Babe Ruth.

TONY. Who does that leave me, Luis Aparicio?

(TONY starts separating the cards. The GUYS gather around the table. BLACKOUT. End of Act I.)

ACT II

Scene 1

MORNING. LIGHT shines in through the windows. FARRAH is sitting in a strapless black dress that's a little too tight for her, eating a bowl of cereal. SHE has a butterfly tattoo on her left shoulder. SHE has on a pearl necklace, large gold earrings, and thick silver bracelets. The stereo is blasting the female rap singer Yo Yo. SHE is moving her head and shoulders to the beat. SHE drops her spoon into the bowl. SHE goes over to the stereo and cranks it up. SHE starts dancing. SHE is right in the groove of the drumbeat, moving her hips, jerking her shoulders.
TONY comes in from the kitchen, dressed in a tuxedo with a red handkerchief in the pocket. HE watches her for a second.

TONY. Uh, excuse me.

(FARRAH dances.)

TONY. Would you mind turning this down?

(FARRAH crouches, gyrating her shoulders to the beat. TONY walks around her to the stereo and turns it off.)

FARRAH. What the fuck?

TONY. This isn't a disco.

FARRAH. Turn it back on.

TONY. It's too early for Hip-hop.

FARRAH. Don't be such an uptight jerkoff.

TONY. Did anyone ever tell you you're a nightmare?

FARRAH. Yeah, my mom, ten times a day for seventeen years. You look hot.

TONY. Do I?

FARRAH. Don't let it go to your head.

TONY. I have to wear a tux in case I win. My agent says it's a lock, but he's been wrong before.

FARRAH. Nervous yet? Personally, I would be shitting bricks. I would be like ... offering my soul to Satan.

TONY. (*Nervously.*) This may seem amazing to you, but there's more important things than the People's Most Popular Award.

FARRAH. Like what? Peace on earth? Why can't you just admit it? Admit you want this award so bad you'd sell your mother for it.

TONY. Where the hell is everybody? Have you seen Lynn?

FARRAH. No. When are we leaving for the awards?

TONY. What do you mean, we?

FARRAH. I mean you, me, and the supporting cast.

TONY. Listen, Farrah, I told Jonny yesterday, I don't have an invitation for you. I'm sorry, but you can't go.

FARRAH. ... What?

TONY. You can't go, Farrah. I'm sorry.

FARRAH. But I'm all dressed up.

TONY. I noticed.

FARRAH. These are real pearls. This is a French dress, and these are fucking Italian shoes. (*SHE clinks her bracelets.*) Silver from Mexico.

TONY. How'd you get all that stuff?

FARRAH. I bought it.

TONY. With what?

FARRAH. I inherited money recently.

TONY. Un-hunh.

FARRAH. Come on, man, take me to the awards. That would be so hot, Patricia at the fucking People's Most Popular Awards. My friends would die like roaches.

TONY. Who's Patricia?

FARRAH. What do you mean, Patricia? Who said Patricia?

TONY. You did.

FARRAH. No I didn't. You're hearing shit.

TONY. Whatever. You can't go, because I don't have a ticket for you. If I had a ticket, I'd give it to you, as long as you didn't sit next to me.

FARRAH. That's a mean thing to say. You think you can go around hurting people's feelings 'cause you're some kind of big deal? Well you're not a big deal, you're just a greedy scumbag like everyone else in this dirty fucking world. I am not a doormat. You got that? People think they can wipe their feet on me, well the next person who wipes his feet on me is gonna get his legs torn off.

(*The PHONE rings.*)

FARRAH. Are you gonna pick up the phone?

TONY. (*Picks up the phone.*) ... Hello? ... Hi. Listen, let me call you back from the car phone, alright? I'd rather speak from the car phone. I'll call you back in a second. In a second, Goddamn it.

(*HE hangs up. The door to the guest bathroom opens and JONNY walks out unsteadily. His eyelids are halfway shut.*)

TONY. There you are. You'd better change, we have to leave soon.

JONNY. ... Change what?

TONY. Your clothing. Do you have anything that doesn't make you look like you're homeless?

JONNY. ... No.

TONY. Alright, who cares, fuck it, it doesn't matter, why am I being so uptight, it's just the People's Most Popular Awards, it's not a funeral. I'll be back in a few minutes, then we'd better go. (*TONY hesitates for a moment.*) Are you stoned?

JONNY. ... Who, me?

TONY. Yeah, you.

JONNY. Couldn't be ... then who? ...

(*TONY gives him a look.*)

TONY. Great. You know if you don't watch out, I'm going to book you into a rehab clinic.

JONNY. Rehab, shmehab. I just need to take a shower ...

TONY. Sounds like a good idea. (*TONY leaves.*)

FARRAH. You're high off your ass, man.

JONNY. ... What?

FARRAH. You're incredibly high.

JONNY. ... Who are you?

FARRAH. What do you mean, who am I? You know who I am.

JONNY. ... No I don't.

FARRAH. You're a waste of space, man. You're a complete waste of bodily fluids.

JONNY. ... Yeah. ... It's true.

FARRAH. Did you boot all the smack?

JONNY. ... No ... I've still got some left.

FARRAH. Well don't boot that up. Maybe you should give it to me to hold.

JONNY. I'm not giving you drugs any more.

FARRAH. Fine, I don't want any.

JONNY. I'm not giving you drugs. You know why?

FARRAH. Because you booted it all last night.

JONNY. ... No ... I'm not ... I'm not giving you drugs ... because ... (*HE fades out.*)

FARRAH. Finish your sentences.

JONNY. ... Because ... you don't like me any more.

FARRAH. I like you. You're alright, except you're a junkie.

JONNY. ... I'm not a junkie.

FARRAH. I've seen junkies before, and you're a junkie.

JONNY. ... That's ... open to debate. (*HE stares into his lap.*) We're through. (*His head drops for a second. HE gives a start, looks over at her.*) We're through ... me and you. Boo hoo. We're through.

FARRAH. That's obvious.

JONNY. Okay. ... I just wanted to make sure.

(*The PHONE rings.*)

JONNY. Telephone.

(With a big effort, HE lifts himself to his feet. LYNN comes in through the kitchen door. SHE is in jeans and a t-shirt. Her hair is uncombed. JONNY exits past her into the hall. The PHONE rings again. LYNN doesn't pick it up.)

FARRAH. Aren't you going to pick it up?
LYNN. It won't be for me.

(The answering machine picks up.)

MACHINE. *(Tony's voice.)* Hi, can't come to the phone right now, so leave a message! Don't hang up! Here comes the beep! ... BEEP.

(The answering machine amplifies the message as it's being recorded.)

MESSAGE. Hi, this is Alexis Thomson, and this is a message for Tony. Tony, you little piece of shit, don't you ever hang up on me again, or I'll cut your balls off. Got that? Thanks.

(The phone is hung up. There is a DIAL TONE for a moment, then the MACHINE CLICKS and REWINDS.)

FARRAH. Was that *the* Alexis Thomson?

(LYNN stands there, staring at the machine.)

FARRAH. Does she always leave messages like that? *(Beat.)* Hello? Anybody home?

(LYNN goes over to the bar. SHE pours some scotch into a glass.)

FARRAH. Pour me one too?

(LYNN sips the scotch. SHE makes a face.)

FARRAH. Nasty, hunh?

(LYNN swallows some more scotch.)

FARRAH. Are you an alcoholic, or is this a special occasion?
LYNN. ... What?
FARRAH. Hey, alright. I was beginning to think I died without realizing it. Ever think that? Maybe you died without knowing it, you still think you're alive, only no one can see or hear you, because you're dead?
LYNN. What time is it?
FARRAH. Twelve thirty. Like this watch? Guess how much it cost. ... Five hundred dollars. This is a five-hundred dollar motherfucking watch. How about that, hunh? ... What's going on, has Tony been hosing Alexis Thomson?
LYNN. Excuse me?

FARRAH. Not to be crude or anything, I was just wondering if your boyfriend's been sleeping with Alexis Thomson or something.

LYNN. What business is it of yours?

FARRAH. It's none of my business.

LYNN. So why don't you shut up?

FARRAH. Okay. (*Beat.*) I wish I was you. ... I look at me, I look at you, and I wish I was you.

LYNN. I wish you were Alexis Thomson.

FARRAH. Why?

LYNN. So I could gouge your eyes out with a fork.

FARRAH. Nice.

LYNN. You know how many times Alexis Thomson has been under the knife? She's had lip injections. A nose job. A butt job. Cheekbones. Breast implants. She's like the bride of Frankenstein, only Alexis isn't as intelligent.

FARRAH. Alexis Thomson had a butt job?

LYNN. Half the people I know have had cosmetic surgery, and the other half are seven years old. I must be out of my mind. What am I doing here? What am I doing with my life?

FARRAH. Don't ask me.

LYNN. I didn't. I forgot you were here.

FARRAH. How could you do that?

LYNN. Easily.

FARRAH. Good answer.

LYNN. ... What's your name again?

FARRAH. Farrah.

LYNN. Right. Farrah. I'm under a lot of stress here. And I don't want to deal with you.

FARRAH. So leave.

LYNN. I live here. This is my house.

FARRAH. "Your" house? Who bought it?

LYNN. ... Tony.

FARRAH. So how is it "your" house?

LYNN. That's a good question.

FARRAH. Not that I blame you.

LYNN. Blame me for what?

FARRAH. Oh, nothing.

LYNN. You think I'm sponging off Tony? Is that what it appears to the outside observer?

FARRAH. I'm not outside. I'm standing right here in the living room. ... Mind if I ask you something?

LYNN. What?

FARRAH. Are you still going?

LYNN. Where?

FARRAH. To the awards. ... The P.M.P. Awards? I just thought after that phone call maybe you didn't wanna go any more.

(LYNN just looks at her.)

FARRAH. You don't know? You're undecided? Well, let me ask you something. If you decide you *don't* want to go, do you think I could have your ticket? ... Whatever. Think about it. It's no big deal, it's just I don't have an invitation.

(TONY hurries in through the front door.)

TONY. *(To Lynn.)* Where have you been? Ready to go? You're not dressed, honey.

FARRAH. Think I'll go try and powder my nose. *(FARRAH gets up and exits.)*

TONY. We'd better get going, sweetie. I was just out in the car, talking to Morty. Where have you been?

LYNN. I went for a walk.

TONY. A walk? Where?

LYNN. I walked down to Sunset Boulevard and back.

TONY. What are you, nuts? Why would you do that?

LYNN. I was thinking about things.

TONY. Un-hunh, anyway, you'd better get changed quickly, where's Fred and Jeff? Doesn't anyone realize we have to get out of here?

LYNN. Tony, we have to talk.

TONY. About what?

LYNN. About our relationship.

TONY. *Now*?

LYNN. Yeah, I think so.

TONY. Lynn, I don't know if you understand what the situation is here.

LYNN. What's the situation?

TONY. The situation is that my show is up for the People's Most Popular Award, and we're scheduled to be at the taping in twenty minutes. I'll be happy to talk with you when we get back, but right now I would appreciate it if you would get changed, because we have to get out of here and over to the theater!

LYNN. So, you were outside talking to Morty, hunh?

TONY. Yeah.

LYNN. That's funny, because Alexis Thomson just called and said if you ever hang up on her again, she was going to cut your balls off.

TONY. Oh yeah, I talked with her too.

LYNN. About what? Did the condom break?

TONY. Lynn, you've got the wrong idea. You see Alexis is having a contract dispute and she thinks I can do something about it. I told her I can't do anything about it, I don't want to be involved in anyone else's contract dispute ... But Alexis is one step away from Charles Manson in terms of being a rational, responsible human being, so she won't take no for answer, in fact she thinks I want her off the show ... this is bullshit.

LYNN. Excuse me?

TONY. This is bullshit. (*Beat.*) I slept with her.

LYNN. You slept with her?

TONY. Once.

(LYNN slaps him across the face.)

LYNN. You pig. You disgusting pig.

TONY. That's not all. (*Beat.*) I slept with Cindy Davis too.

LYNN. What?

TONY. I also slept once with Cindy Davis. But it wasn't fun.

(LYNN gets up.)

TONY. But I'll tell you the real truth. I would have both of them rubbed out. I would chop them both up into chum and feed them to the sharks if I thought it would help me get you back.

LYNN. Why?

TONY. Because you're kind, and innocent, and you loved me before I became successful, and you and my friends are the only thing that I can see building a future on.

LYNN. Tony, you don't know anything about me.

(LYNN exits up the stairs. TONY looks up after her, then HE goes over to the machine. His hand reaches out, as if he is not controlling it, and HE pushes the playback button. The machine rewinds and plays the message.)

MESSAGE. Hi, this is Alexis Thomson, and this is a message for Tony. Tony, you little piece of shit, don't you ever hang up on me again, or I'll cut your balls off. Got that? Thanks.

(TONY retreats to the couch. HE stands there for a moment, his shoulders hunched up. Suddenly HE has a sort of spasm, his body contorting violently with a shudder. JEFF comes in from the hall. TONY calms himself.)

JEFF. Are you alright?

TONY. Yeah, where have you been?

JEFF. In my room.

TONY. We have to get going, is Fred ready?

JEFF. I don't know.

TONY. Don't you want to change?

JEFF. Uh, I can't. Remember? My suitcase got sent to Paris.

TONY. Oh, yeah. Well never mind, you look fine.

JEFF. Tony, I think there's something I should talk with you about.

TONY. Yes, Jeff?

JEFF. Well, this is really hard for me to say. I've been thinking about it all morning, and I feel as if I'm here under ... false pretenses.

TONY. Un-hunh. (*TONY looks at his watch.*)

JEFF. I think I just have to be honest with you. Tony, ever since senior year of college, when I came up and ... visited you for a week, I've had a ... crush on Lynn. No, that's not true. It isn't a crush. I fell in love with her. And it hasn't gone away. When you called to invite me out here, the first thought in my mind was: Lynn. I'm going to get to see Lynn again. I guess I'm still in love with her. I don't know why. I wish I could make it go away. But it won't.

TONY. (*Nods.*) Uh, that's ... that's great, Jeff.

JEFF. I haven't spoken to her about it. I have no reason to think she ... reciprocates these feelings in any way. Basically the whole thing exists inside my own head. (*HE stands there.*)

TONY. Are you finished?

JEFF. Yes, except to say that I'm ... truly sorry.

(*TONY looks at his watch. HE smiles.*)

JEFF. You're smiling. Why are you smiling?

TONY. I'm just wondering if there's some sort of conspiracy to fuck up my life this morning.

JEFF. I'm sorry, Tony. I'm sorry.

TONY. Stop saying you're sorry. Where is Fred?

JEFF. I don't know.

TONY. FRED?! LET'S GET GOING!

JEFF. I ... I can understand your reaction to this, I can understand that you must feel like throwing me out of your house. All I can say in my defense is that I haven't brought this up with Lynn. Not that my reasons for not speaking to Lynn are pure, that would be a misrepresentation. The fact is that I'm too afraid to speak to her. What if she laughed at me? What if I told her everything, and she burst into hysterical laughter? I'm not sure I could recover from a blow like that. In a way, this whole thing is just a symptom of my biggest problem in life, which is that I'm afraid. I'm horribly afraid, Tony. I'm afraid of things having no meaning, and even more than that, I'm afraid of them having meaning. I'm a terrible hypochondriac. Sometimes I sit in my room and worry for hours on end that I have AIDS, despite the fact that I've never had intercourse. I can't take action. Once I thought that by studying hard and getting straight A's, I was taking action. I used to bring in my report cards to my mother's study, and she'd go over them, with this serious expression on her face, ever since I remember, that was what I did when my report card arrived. Last year when I got my final grades, she was in the hospital. I brought my grades in for her to look at in the hospital room. She was numb from pain-killers. She sort of took the transcript and held it in her hand, and smiled. She didn't even know what it was, I think. And I stood there and thought, "Who am I?" I began to plummet, I was falling and falling, standing there in that hospital room with nothing to hold on to. I ... I need to take action, Tony. I need to take some sort of action.

(FARRAH'S VOICE is heard from the hall.)

FARRAH. Hey, would someone give me a hand here?

(FARRAH comes in, half-dragging, half-walking JONNY. JONNY's legs are wobbly. FARRAH has his arm around her shoulder. SHE is bent over by his weight. For a moment EVERYONE just watches.)

FARRAH. I can't carry him.

(JEFF hurries over and grabs Jonny's other arm. THEY make their way to the couch, with JONNY sagging between them.)

FARRAH. I found him on the floor.
TONY. What's wrong with him?
FARRAH. What do you think?
JEFF. Is he sick?
FARRAH. He's OD-ing.
TONY. What do you mean, he's OD-ing?

(LYNN comes down the stairs.)

FARRAH. He's been booting all night, and he just went and booted the last of the heroin. I don't know how much was left.
TONY. What do you mean, he "booted" it? would you speak English, please?
FARRAH. He's been shooting up all night.
JEFF. Like with a hypodermic?
FARRAH. Well he didn't use a bicycle pump.
TONY. He's been shooting up?
LYNN. Is he okay?
JEFF. Are you alright, Fred?
TONY. I can't fucking believe this.

JEFF. Fred? Fred, are you alright?

(There is a pause as EVERYONE waits for Jonny to answer. JONNY starts making a croaking noise as HE sucks in air. The sound is horrible, like someone belching in reverse.)

TONY. Oh, Jesus—
LYNN. What's that sound he's making?
FARRAH. He's trying to breathe.
TONY. What do you mean, he's trying to breathe?
FARRAH. I mean he's trying to breathe, what the fuck do you think I mean?
JEFF. Well what do we do?
FARRAH. I've only seen this once before, but I think we have to keep him moving.
TONY. GET UP. GET UP, FRED.
FARRAH. That ain't gonna do it. We have to, like, walk him around.

(JEFF and TONY grab JONNY and hoist him up onto his feet. JONNY moans. JEFF starts walking, with JONNY sagging off to the side.)

JEFF. Walk, man, walk! Tony, grab his other arm.
TONY. I can't believe this!

(THEY walk with Jonny, half-carrying him.)

TONY. You stupid asshole. You stupid asshole.
LYNN. Is he breathing?

(THEY pause for a second. JONNY is not making the croaking sound any more.)

JEFF. Yeah, he's breathing.
FARRAH. Keep walking him around.
JEFF. He's heavy.
TONY. We don't have time for this.

(THEY walk in a circle around the couch.)

TONY. How long should we do this for?
FARRAH. As long as you can.
TONY. As long as we can?
LYNN. I'm going to call an ambulance.
TONY. An ambulance? Do you think we should?

(HE lets go of Jonny's arm. JEFF tries to keep him moving.)

JEFF. Hey, Tony!
LYNN. You don't think I should call an ambulance?
TONY. Maybe he doesn't need an ambulance. *(To Farrah.)* Does he need an ambulance?
FARRAH. How the fuck should I know?
JEFF. I think he's trying to say something.
TONY. What?! What?!
JONNY. *(Mumbles.)* No ambulance.
TONY. No ambulance? You don't want an ambulance?

(THEY all look at Jonny. HE begins to croak for breath again.)

TONY. I think we should call an ambulance.
LYNN. I'm calling an ambulance.
TONY. Go ahead!
LYNN. I am!
FARRAH. We should put ice down his pants.
JEFF. Are you serious?
FARRAH. Yeah, anything to keep him breathing. I'll get some ice. Keep walking him around. (*FARRAH exits into the kitchen.*)
JEFF. Tony, help me.

(*TONY comes over to Jonny and holds his face.*)

TONY. Hey, Fred, listen, Fred, cut the shit. Snap out of it, man, okay? (*JONNY's head sags.*) Hey, Fred, Fred! (*TONY slaps him in the face.*) Listen, you asshole, you cannot die, alright? We have to stick together now, you hear me? We've got plans to make! So snap out of it before I kick your ass, alright!
JEFF. Tony, I don't know how productive this is.

(*FARRAH comes out of the kitchen.*)

FARRAH. Okay, I've got some ice.
TONY. Drop it down his pants.
FARRAH. Hold him up.
LYNN. I called the ambulance.
FARRAH. Shit! (*FARRAH is trying to unbutton his pants with her free hand.*)
LYNN. What are you doing?

FARRAH. I'm gonna give him a blowjob—what do you think I'm doing, I'm putting ice down his pants. (*SHE drops the ice into Jonny's underwear.*) Okay, bull's-eye.

TONY. Hey, Fred, wake up!

JEFF. Wake up, Fred!

FARRAH. Come on, Jonny!

JEFF. Fred! Come on, Fred!

(At first JONNY has no reaction. Then HE moans softly, and tries to shake his leg in slow motion.)

FARRAH. You'd better keep him moving.

JEFF. Alright, Tony, let's go.

(THEY start staggering around again.)

JEFF. Does anyone here know CPR?

FARRAH. No.

LYNN. No.

TONY. Of course not.

(THEY circle the couch.)

TONY. This is a nightmare. This is a fucking nightmare. We have to get out of here. How long did they say the ambulance would take?

LYNN. I don't know.

TONY. Didn't you ask?

LYNN. They said it would come as soon as possible.

TONY. As soon as possible, hunh? Well where the fuck are they?

LYNN. I just called.

TONY. What time is it? What time is it? (*HE looks at his watch.*) Jesus Christ.

LYNN. Tony, if you want to go, then go. (*SHE steps in and grabs Jonny's arm, replacing Tony.*)

TONY. What are you doing?

LYNN. I'll walk him around until the ambulance comes.

TONY. I can't just go.

LYNN. We don't all have to stay here.

TONY. Yeah, but ...

JEFF. Yeah, Tony, you might as well go on ahead.

TONY. Shouldn't I wait?

LYNN. You'll miss the taping if you wait.

(*LYNN and JEFF are walking JONNY around in a circle.*)

JEFF. Go ahead, man.

TONY. Will you come meet me there once he's okay?

JEFF. Sure.

TONY. Lynn—Lynn, will you meet me there?

LYNN. Yeah, alright.

TONY. Because we have to talk, okay? I want to talk with you.

LYNN. Fine.

TONY. Well, alright, alright, I guess I could ...

FARRAH. Wait, I'll go with you!

TONY. I'll call you—I'll call you from the car, okay?

JEFF. Okay, man.

TONY. Right ... (*TONY exits through the front door.*)

FARRAH. Well, fuck it. Guess I'm not going.

LYNN. Come on, let's keep him walking.

(THEY start circling the couch with JONNY. BLACKOUT.)

Scene 2

The TELEPHONE rings abrasively. LIGHTS UP.

FARRAH. Telephone.

(It's late afternoon. JEFF is sitting on the couch with a cup of coffee. HE's in one of Tony's shirts. FARRAH is still in her tight dress. The PHONE rings again.)

FARRAH. Am I the only one who can pick up the phone here? (*FARRAH picks up the phone.*) Hello? ... No, he's not. ... Yeah, sure. Hold on one second. (*SHE picks up a pen.*) Alright, what's your name again? Mike Arxvardzd? How do you spell that? A-r-x-v-a-r-d-z-d. From HBO? I'll put you on the list. Hey, you need any actresses over there? ... Hello? (*SHE looks at the phone a second, then hangs up.*) Asshole ... Did it sound like I was joking? I could be an actress. Wanna see me a ˙?

JEFF. I don't know.

FARRAH. Alright, ready? (*SH
appropriate, and seemingly since*
love you. I really love you. ... I I
Easy now, hand over that gun
something just fall down into my
and give me a kiss. ... You slimy

you if you were the last person left on this stinking planet!
... What do you think?

JEFF. I guess you could be an actress.

FARRAH. Of course I'd rather direct. But a lot of actors
are moving into directing nowadays, right?

*(JEFF nods into his coffee. FARRAH sits down on the
couch. For a moment, BOTH of them are silent. JEFF
broods. FARRAH picks at a string on the couch.)*

FARRAH. Has Tony ever said anything about me?

JEFF. Not that I can remember.

FARRAH. Nothing?

JEFF. *(Thinks.)* No.

FARRAH. Oh. *(SHE tries to pull down the hem of her
dress, but it's impossible.)* I think he doesn't like me. Has
he ever said anything like that? That he doesn't like me?

JEFF. I can't remember him saying anything at all
about you.

FARRAH. Why doesn't he like me? Is it the way I
dress, the way I act, what?

(JEFF shrugs.)

FARRAH. This dress is too short, isn't it? Fuckin'
dress. No wonder he didn't want to take me to the awards.
(Beat.) Wish I owned this place. I'd buy a shotgun. That's
security, hunh? A nice house and a shotgun. *(SHE gets
up.)* Think I'm going to change. What do you think? Is
is dress too much, or what? I mean in the past I've
d that nothing is too much, but I don't know any
ybe this dress is too much. Or is it sexy? Should

I stick with this dress, or should I change into something casual? Do I look like an asshole in this dress? I need help here. I can't figure out what to wear. I just can't decide. I can't fucking decide. What's happening to me? I'm wavering. I'd better not be wavering. I can't let this shit happen to me. First you can't decide one little thing, like what dress to wear, and the next thing you know, you can't decide anything, and you have a nervous fucking breakdown. I've seen it happen.

JEFF. Change into something else.

FARRAH. Yeah? You think so?

JEFF. At least then you'll feel like you're doing something. Even if you're actually doing nothing.

FARRAH. That makes sense. Okay, thanks a lot.

(JONNY comes in slowly from the hall. HE squints his eyes against the light. HE looks sick.)

JONNY. I told you not to call an ambulance.

FARRAH. It's the creature from the black lagoon.

JONNY. What time is it?

JEFF. About five thirty.

JONNY. Phone keeps ringing.

JEFF. Everyone's calling to congratulate Tony.

JONNY. For what?

JEFF. You know, that thing.

FARRAH. How are you feeling?

JONNY. Excuse me?

FARRAH. How are you?

JONNY. Why do you ask?

FARRAH. I don't know, because you almost just croaked, I guess.

JONNY. Sorry to disappoint you.

FARRAH. Oh grow up, man. I can't believe you're still bummed out that I dumped you.

JONNY. Did you dump me? I hadn't realized.

FARRAH. It's not like we were engaged to be married. Look, I'm sorry. I'm sorry I dumped you. But we only went out for three weeks, alright? We never even said we were going out. I am not the bad guy in this situation. I hate when people try and twist shit around and blame everything on me. (*FARRAH exits down the hall.*)

JONNY. (*Groans.*) Oooooh.

JEFF. You should have let them take you to the hospital.

JONNY. I was fine.

JEFF. Just because you're able to say "I'm okay" over and over again doesn't mean you're fine.

JONNY. I don't have health insurance. So I'm not going to any hospital.

JEFF. You don't have health insurance?

JONNY. Why would I need health insurance?

JEFF. You almost asphyxiated.

JONNY. No I didn't.

JEFF. You threw up for an hour and a half after they left.

JONNY. Sorry about your shirt.

JEFF. That's alright. I took a new one out of Tony's drawer.

JONNY. You have some cash with you?

JEFF. Cash? Why?

JONNY. I need to borrow gas money to get back to San Francisco.

JEFF. When are you going?

JONNY. Now. I have to be back to work by tomorrow morning. Could you lend me like ... a hundred fifty bucks?

JEFF. A hundred fifty bucks for gas?

JONNY. Not just for gas. I need a tire. My right rear tire is fucked, I'm afraid it's not gonna make it all the way.

JEFF. Listen, uh ... Fred. I want to ... I want to talk with you about something. Why don't you ... sit down.

JONNY. I don't want to sit down.

JEFF. Okay. Uh ... this is not easy for me to talk about.

JONNY. Then don't talk about it.

JEFF. Uh, well ...

JONNY. Will you lend me the money?

JEFF. I think ... you need to like ... get some help.

JONNY. Jeff, I know you're trying to do me a favor, but the best thing you can do is lend me the money so I can get out of here.

JEFF. I don't think so. No. I'm not going to lend you cash.

JONNY. Come on. You'll get it back. I swear to God you will. I'll send it within the week. It's just I thought I brought more money than I actually did. I have two wallets, and I took the wrong one. I took the brown one. I should have taken the black one.

(LYNN comes down the stairs, carrying a small suitcase.)

JONNY. Lynn, Lynn, can I borrow some money?

LYNN. No.

JONNY. Come on, I'll pay you back, I can send it tomorrow, Federal Express. I promise. I have to get back, or I'll be fired. They'll give my job to someone with the advantage of no education. Come on, Lynn.

LYNN. I need my money.

JONNY. Alright. Forget it. Just forget it. (*HE exits.*)

JEFF. Are you going somewhere?

LYNN. How did you know?

JEFF. You have a suitcase in your hand.

LYNN. Oh, right. I'm a little nervous. ... I'm just going to put this in the front closet. (*SHE puts the suitcase in the front closet.*) Okay, it's in the front closet. (*SHE comes back. Stands in the middle of the room.*) Christ.

JEFF. What?

LYNN. I've lived here for two years. I've lived in this house for two years.

JEFF. It's a ... nice house.

LYNN. Yes.

JEFF. The rooms are ... big. The pool's ...

LYNN. The pool's great.

JEFF. The flowers. The trees.

LYNN. It's a Japanese gardener. He does Patrick Swayze.

JEFF. Who?

LYNN. Patrick Swayze. He's an actor.

JEFF. Oh. ... You must think I'm retarded.

LYNN. No, I don't think you're retarded. (*LYNN takes out a Marlboro and lights it.*)

JEFF. I didn't know you smoked.

LYNN. I'm planning on taking it up again.

JEFF. Why?

LYNN. Who cares? (*SHE inhales.*) Excuse me. I'm just a little flustered.

JEFF. Why?

LYNN. Because I would prefer to just leave, but I can't.

JEFF. Leave where? (*Beat.*) Wait a minute, you mean uh ... I mean ... you're saying ...

LYNN. I can't just leave a note. Although that would be a lot easier.

JEFF. So then, uh ... Tony and you ... I mean ... the thing uh ...

LYNN. Jeff ...

JEFF. What?

LYNN. You're muttering to yourself.

JEFF. Am I?

LYNN. You do it all the time.

JEFF. Yeah, I know. I guess I'm afraid if ... I articulate myself, people will actually ... hear what I'm saying, and I'll be held accountable for it.

LYNN. If you have something to say, just say it. The world isn't going to cave in. (*SHE sits down.*) In theory at least. ... I'm exhausted. My shoulders. (*SHE looks over at Jeff.*) Sorry, I'll go back upstairs and wait.

JEFF. You know ... my mother was a teacher.

LYNN. Was she?

JEFF. Yeah. Well, a Professor ... She lectured in ethics. She used to say that ... Hell is the reverberation of all the wrong actions taken in life.

LYNN. When would she say that?

JEFF. Oh, you know, at the dinner table. Whenever.

LYNN. That's harsh.

JEFF. She was a real ... disciplinarian when I was little. So I always ... worried about, you know, making a wrong action. But ... she was cool, I mean ... She had to deal ... on her own. My father committed suicide when I was seven years old. Not because of my mother, don't get me wrong, it was more ... because of *his* mother.

LYNN. I'm sorry.

JEFF. No, don't be sorry. *I'm* sorry, I don't know ... why I started talking about it. It's not very ... appropriate. I apologize.

LYNN. You don't have to apologize.

JEFF. You're right, I'm sorry.

LYNN. You're apologizing for apologizing.

JEFF. (*Laughs.*) That's me, there, in a nutshell ... So, do you think you'll ... continue with teaching?

LYNN. Me? ... Yes. But ... I want to keep teaching kids. I'm finding adults less and less interesting. Of course in terms of.. money and prestige, being a teacher is on a par with being a lavatory attendant, but so what, this society is perverse.

JEFF. Yeah, I guess ... sometimes I get these thoughts ... that I should maybe ... quit law and become a painter and teach art to emotionally disturbed kids.

(LYNN looks at him.)

JEFF. I don't know, I ... I always liked drawing and painting, and ... I think I'd have a lot of patience dealing with emotionally disturbed kids. I think I could identify with them. I mean, you know ... to an extent. I'd be interested to ... talk to you about teaching sometime.

LYNN. ... I don't teach emotionally disturbed kids. At least the system doesn't classify them as emotionally disturbed. But a lot of them have had some kind of abuse, either physical or mental. It's hard. It's very hard for them to pay attention.

JEFF. I'm in love with you.

LYNN. ... What?

JEFF. Excuse me? ...

LYNN. ... I thought you said something.

JEFF. ... No, no, I didn't say anything. (*Beat.*) Yes I did, I did, I said I'm in love with you. I think I've been in love with you from the first moment I laid eyes on you. I remember exactly what you were wearing, black jeans and a red sweater and silver loop earrings, not that my attraction is a physical one, I mean it is physical, but it's more than that, it's mental and spiritual, I think you're a moral person and a noble one, and I respect the fact that you're a teacher, and I like your sense of humor, and I don't mean to put you in an awkward position but I can't keep it in my chest any longer. I love you.

(*The front door opens and TONY comes in.*)

TONY. I won. I won the stupid fucking People's Most Popular Award! This changes everything!—These are for you, honey. (*HE hands Lynn a box of flowers.*) Thank God Fred's okay. Is he still asleep?

LYNN. Uh ...

TONY. I've got to talk to him. I've got the solution. (*TONY takes off his jacket.*) I met Michael Jackson. He watches the show, can you believe it? He invited us over for some hot chocolate. (*TONY laughs.*) He said, "You should come over for some hot chocolate." You want to go to Michael Jackson's for hot chocolate?

LYNN. No.

TONY. You really missed something. Sammie Hector, the actor without any arms and legs was sitting right in front of me. He was in a custom-made purple tuxedo and sunglasses. "Love your show, babe," he said to me. But most importantly—check this out, Jeff! Chip Goldberg— Chip Goldberg comes up to my agent Morty after the show, and says we've got a deal. "Who's Chip Goldberg?" you might ask. Well, Chip Goldberg is Universal TV. In other words, in other words, I think we're in business, Jeff. I think All For One Productions is becoming a reality. And all because of this. (*TONY takes out the People's Most Popular Award. It's a gold colored disc on a stick.*) The People's Most Popular Award. Made in Taiwan. I think I'll mount it on the hood of the Porsche.

 JEFF. I'm in love with you.
 TONY. Excuse me?

(JEFF gets down on his knees in front of Lynn.)

 JEFF. I'm in love with you, Lynn.

(TONY stares at Jeff.)

 TONY. Jeff, what are you doing?
 JEFF. I'm taking action, Tony.
 TONY. You're taking acid?
 JEFF. Action. I'm taking action.
 LYNN. Please get up, Jeff.
 JEFF. (*To Lynn.*) I'm in love with you.
 TONY. You're not in love with her.
 JEFF. Yes I am.
 TONY. You're not. And you know why? Because you're my oldest friend. And we've got work to do. Now get the hell up off your knees.

JEFF. (*To Lynn.*) You don't need to give me any response.

LYNN. Jeff, please get up.

TONY. You're making an ass of yourself.

LYNN. Shut up, Tony.

TONY. "Shut up"? I'm not the guy who's telling his oldest friend's girlfriend he's in love with her. I mean I'm in love with you too, okay?

LYNN. No you're not.

TONY. Can we—can we discuss this in private, please?

JEFF. Just being able to tell you is enough for me.

TONY. Jeff, for Christ's sake, have you had a stroke or something? Would you please behave yourself?

LYNN. Please get up off your knees, Jeff.

JEFF. Okay. (*JEFF gets up.*) Lynn, I hope you'll ... excuse my self-indulgence.

TONY. You hope she'll excuse it?

LYNN. Tony, I'm leaving you.

TONY. You're what?

JEFF. She's leaving you, Tony.

TONY. Yeah, I heard it the first time.

LYNN. You'll be fine, Tony. You've worked really hard and ... I'm sure you're going to be a big success.

TONY. We don't know that. I mean ... I'm not just going to produce stuff like Model Detectives. I'm also ... going to do spin-offs of Model Detectives—I'm only kidding. I'm going to ... I'm actually going to make intelligent shows, I think maybe you'll be proud of the stuff I'm capable of doing in the future—

LYNN. That's great, that's great, Tony, but that's your life. I'm a teacher, I've got college loans to pay off. I'm going to ... I'm going to get a little apartment in a ... in a dangerous neighborhood, probably, I'll ... live with a couple of other teachers who are ... equally impoverished ... we'll ... cook spaghetti a lot, I won't eat out every night, I'll ... I'll eat spaghetti and tomato sauce, like ... a normal person, I'll talk about ... things I want to talk about, like ... Stephen Washington, who I'm ... I'm convinced he's dyslexic, despite the fact that the school refuses to diagnose him as such, and I'll ... I'll be really lonely without you, Tony, but ... I'm lonely anyway, I'm lonely right now, so it'll be ... it'll be okay.

TONY. You're leaving me so you can eat spaghetti?

LYNN. No, Tony—

JEFF. She's leaving you because you slept with two other women.

LYNN. How did you know that?

JEFF. He told me.

LYNN. You told him? What were you, bragging about it?

TONY. No! No, I wasn't bragging, Jesus! Would you tell her, Jeff?

JEFF. He wasn't bragging. But still—

LYNN. I've got to get out of here.

TONY. It didn't mean anything, Lynn.

LYNN. I know. Let's not confuse things. The fact that you ... did whatever you did with those two creatures ... is irrelevant. Completely irrelevant. I can't let myself get caught up in that.

TONY. Listen, Lynn, I've been ... I've been thinking ... maybe I could, you know. Maybe you'd let me pay off your loans for you.

LYNN. Tony, are you ... trying to bribe me?

TONY. No, of course not. I'm just ... telling you that I love you, I love you, I'm not sure who I am ... who I would be without you. So ... I guess what I'm saying is ... will you marry me?

LYNN. You're asking me to marry you? Tony, you don't listen to me. I don't even love you any more.

TONY. Pardon me?

LYNN. I don't love you any more. I feel trapped. I'm leaving. Sorry. (*LYNN goes to the front closet and takes out her suitcase.*)

TONY. Don't leave.

JEFF. Where are you going?

LYNN. I'm going to stay for a while at Ellie Mcdonald's.

TONY. Who's Ellie Mcdonald?

LYNN. You know who Ellie is.

TONY. No, I don't.

LYNN. She teaches section 3C.

TONY. Oh yeah ... Right.

LYNN. Well. I don't know what else to say.

JEFF. Can I call you?

LYNN. Jeff ... maybe. In a few months.

TONY. You're letting him call you?

LYNN. I just want to be alone. For a while. Quite a while.

JEFF. Where can I reach you? At work? At your friend's house?

TONY. Jeff, if you don't shut up, I'm going to hit you really hard in the face.

LYNN. Tony ...

TONY. (*Hangs his head.*) Don't leave.

LYNN. ... I'll have to pick up my stuff sometime.

TONY. Don't leave.

LYNN. Give me your hand. (*SHE hands him the earring box.*) The earrings.

TONY. The what?

LYNN. The earrings you gave me.

TONY. Keep them.

LYNN. I can't.

TONY. Please keep them.

LYNN. ... No. I don't want them.

*(THEY stand there looking at each other.
JEFF watches them.)*

LYNN. Deep breath. (*SHE kisses Tony softly on the lips.*) 'Bye, Tony.

*(Then SHE leaves.
TONY stands there a few seconds.
Then HE follows her out.)*

TONY. Lynn—

(HE exits. Overcome, JEFF lies down on the floor. JONNY comes out from the hallway. HE sees Tony's jacket. HE looks around, doesn't see Jeff. HE rifles Tony's pockets. HE pulls out Tony's wallet from an inside pocket. HE opens it and takes the cash out. HE's breathing quickly. HE shoves the cash into his pocket. JEFF looks up.)

JEFF. Fred? What are you doing?

(JONNY jumps from fright, dropping the wallet. TONY comes in, looking miserable.)

JONNY. Heeeeeeeey, To-NY! Al-RIGHT! *(JONNY pretends to be announcing a prize-fight.)* And the winner is ... BIG TONY! *(JONNY imitates the roar of the crowd.)* Roooar ... Roooar ... Yeaaaaah ... Whooooo ...

JEFF. Is that Tony's wallet?

JONNY. What, this? Oh, yeah, I found your wallet. *(HE hands Tony his wallet.)*

JEFF. Tony, he took money from your wallet.

JONNY. No, I didn't, there wasn't any money in there.

JEFF. Was there, Tony?

TONY. Uh ...

JONNY. Hey, fuck you guys, alright? You think I would steal money from you? Well fuck you. ... I'm getting out of here.

TONY. Fred, I can't believe this.

JONNY. I didn't take anything from you.

JEFF. I saw you!

JONNY. Leave me alone! What's a hundred bucks to you, you Hebe!

TONY. "You Hebe"? Fred, I'm Protestant. You're Jewish.

JONNY. It's an expression! *(JONNY starts towards the door.)*

JEFF. Where are you going?

JONNY. Home.

JEFF. No you're not.

JONNY. Get outta my way!

JEFF. Fred, you're an addict—

JONNY. I'm not an addict!

TONY. Yes you are—
JONNY. I didn't steal shit!
JEFF. Then pull out your pocket—
JONNY. No!

(JEFF and TONY grab him to stop him from going out.)

JEFF. Uh, guys—
JONNY. Get off! Get away!

(THEY struggle. JONNY shoves his fist down into his pocket. JEFF tries to pull it out.)

JONNY. Get off, you pervert! I hate you! I hate you! Get off! *(JONNY shoves Jeff, and the cash comes fluttering down onto the carpet. JONNY gets down on his hands and knees, scooping them up, shoving them into his pockets. Then HE stops.)* Oh, shit. *(JONNY drops the bills he's holding.)* Oh, shit. *(JONNY groans.)* Oh, man, no. Please, please, no. *(JONNY looks at his hands.)* Please, please. Don't tell me. Please. I'm not an addict. *(HE starts crying.)* I'm a fucking addict. I can't help myself. I'm an addict.

(TONY and JEFF watch him.)

JONNY. I'm sorry. I'm sorry. I didn't mean anything. I didn't mean anything bad.
TONY. It's alright.
JEFF. *(Puts his hand on Jonny's shoulder.)* It's alright, man.
JONNY. I have to puke.

JEFF. Uh, wait—

(JEFF steps back. JONNY dry-heaves.)

JONNY. I can't even puke. There's nothing in my stomach. *(HE spits.)* I can't even puke. *(HE wipes his mouth.)* I'm useless.

JEFF. Listen, Fred, uh ... you're a good person. I've known you since you were seven ... and ... you're intelligent, and creative, and ... a good person.

JONNY. It's ... Jonny ... I really did have it ... legally changed.

TONY. I made an appointment for you at a rehab clinic.

JONNY. You what?

JEFF. You did?

TONY. Yeah. *(Beat.)* I had my assistant call. We sent one of the actors earlier in the season. They're expecting you guys this afternoon.

JEFF. I don't need to go to rehab.

TONY. But you'll take him, won't you? You'll drive him over there.

JEFF. Uh ... sure. Fred, we'll uh ... call your parents.

JONNY. My parents? They're worried about whether I'm eating enough vegetables. If they knew about this ...

(TONY hands a photocopied sheet of paper to JEFF.)

TONY. These are directions to the clinic. *(TONY picks a twenty off the floor.)* This is for gas. Jonny, if you need anything, you can have them call my assistant Tracy. They have the number there. *(TONY folds the rest of the money and puts it in his pocket.)* You'd better get going.

(JONNY stands up unsteadily.)

JONNY. I don't know, man. (*HE wipes his nose.*) Rehab? ... That wasn't exactly part of my thirteen point plan for stardom.

TONY. You know how many stars go to this clinic? You'll probably make some great connections.

JONNY. You mean like ... I'll be dry-heaving next to Liz Taylor?

TONY. And Keith Richards.

JEFF. You'll probably ... start a band with him.

JONNY. No, I'm a solo artist.

JEFF. Are you going to come, Tony?

TONY. No.

JONNY. Wait a minute, I haven't said I'd go yet.

TONY. Listen, shithead, there's no debate. You're going.

JONNY. Uh ... okay.

(Beat.)

JEFF. So you're ... you're not coming, Tony? (*Beat.*) Are you uh ... angry with me about the uh ... Lynn thing?

TONY. "The Lynn thing"? (*Beat.*) It didn't have anything to do with you.

JONNY. What Lynn thing?

JEFF. I uh ... made a pass at Lynn.

TONY. A pass? You practically lit yourself on fire.

JONNY. Far out.

TONY. You guys ... you guys are really from Mars, you know that?

JONNY. Take me to your leader. (*Beat.*) Tony, I'm sorry I called you a Hebe.

TONY. That's alright. (*Neat.*) Remember what you used to call me?

JONNY. No, what?

TONY. You used to call me fartbreath. (*Beat.*) In first grade.

JONNY. I did?

JEFF. And what was it you used to call me?

TONY. Tit-cheeks.

JEFF. Oh, yeah.

JONNY. So you mean I've always been like this.

TONY. Okay, take care, guys. (*TONY sticks out his hand.*)

JEFF. Now I ... feel like a jerk.

TONY. No, I'm the jerk.

JONNY. We're all jerks. But we're so good-looking that it doesn't matter.

(THEY shake hands.)

JONNY. I guess this means the guest spot is definitely off. (*Beat.*) Okay, Tony. I'm sorry I O.D.'d in your house.

(Beat.)

JEFF. So maybe I'll ... call you sometime.

TONY. Yeah.

JONNY. See you, Tony.

TONY. Yeah. Yeah, I'll see you guys.

(THEY hesitate for a moment, the THREE OF THEM looking at each other. Then JONNY and JEFF leave.
TONY picks up the phone. HE puts it back down. HE walks to the flowers. HE walks to the bar. HE sits in front of his Strat-o-matic Baseball game and picks up the dice.)

TONY. Hack Wilson at the plate. The pitch. *(HE puts the card up to his mouth.)* Ah, fuck—

(HE starts to cry. FARRAH walks in, in jeans and a t-shirt.)

FARRAH. Hey, Tony! Congratulations!

(TONY pulls himself together. Looks at her.)

TONY. Thanks.
FARRAH. Incredible, man. I knew you would win.
TONY. Thanks a lot.
FARRAH. Is this it? *(SHE picks up the award.)* Looks sort of cheap. ... Are you okay?
TONY. Sure.
FARRAH. Where is everyone?
TONY. They left. Lynn, you remember Lynn?
FARRAH. Yeah, I remember her.
TONY. She left. She left me.
FARRAH. Far out.
TONY. I slept with two other women.
FARRAH. You big horn-dog. Where are your friends?
TONY. They left too.
FARRAH. They did, hunh?

TONY. I don't have any friends.

FARRAH. After a certain point, I think we outgrow friendship.

TONY. I don't know what to do. I don't have anyone to talk to.

FARRAH. What about your parents?

TONY. Did they call?

FARRAH. No, but a lot of other people did.

TONY. My parents didn't call?

FARRAH. Nope. Oh, well. What are parents? They're just two people who screwed one night and then decided not to have an abortion.

TONY. You have a great way with words.

FARRAH. Well, how about me? You could talk to me.

TONY. You're insane.

FARRAH. Yeah, but I'm here. Everyone else seems to have blown you off.

TONY. True.

FARRAH. But you should expect that. That's what happens to people like you and me. It's like the dinosaurs. Some of them were plant-eaters, some were meat-eaters. We're meat-eaters. You expect the other ones to hang around with us?

TONY. I'm not a meat-eater.

FARRAH. Sure you are. I could smell you a mile off. I know you. I know you because you're just like me.

TONY. I'm not like you. Whatever you are, I'm not like you.

FARRAH. Look, I don't have to tell you this shit. It would be a lot easier for me to say, "Oh, poor baby, your friends all left you." I'd probably get what I want a lot easier that way.

TONY. What do you want?

FARRAH. I want to stay here. I want to stay in your house.

TONY. Why, Farrah? Don't you have a home? Don't you live anywhere?

FARRAH. No I don't. I don't have any money, I don't have any place to stay. I do have six pairs of Italian shoes that I charged up on my mom's boyfriend's credit card, that dirty letch. But it doesn't matter, I could have nothing and I'd still make it, because I'm a carnivore. Everyone else better watch out. (*Beat.*) What do you say, man, can I stay here? I won't steal anything. I wouldn't get away with it. I just need a place to shack up. This is such a big house, you wouldn't even have to see me. I could just stay in my room and watch TV. You gotta let me stay. I'll do anything, man. I'm serious. I'll do *anything*.

TONY. You don't have to do anything.

FARRAH. You mean I can stay?

TONY. Yeah.

FARRAH. For as long as I like?

TONY. Farrah, don't push it.

FARRAH. (*Breathes a heavy sigh.*) Fuckin' A, man. That's a load off my mind. (*SHE sits down on the couch.*) ... I don't want to have sex with you.

(*TONY looks over at her.*)

FARRAH. You said I didn't have to.

TONY. Did I mention sex?

FARRAH. Not that you're hideous or anything. I just really don't want to have sex with you.

TONY. That's fine. I don't want to have sex with you, either.

FARRAH. Really? (*Beat.*) This is going pretty good so far. (*Beat.*) So what was it like?

TONY. What?

FARRAH. You know. When they announced the winner.

TONY. Oh ... it was silly.

FARRAH. Silly?

TONY. It's not really worth going into.

FARRAH. What are you, gonna make me beg for it?

TONY. Loni Anderson presented the award ... She read the names of all the nominated shows, and my heart was ... beating faster and faster. The audience was silent, I heard her say, "And the winner is ..." and I looked over at my agent, Morty, our eyes met, and he had this expression on his face, this expression of ... of ... fear. It was an expression of fear. Absolute fear. It was like I got a glimpse into his soul. And then I heard "Model Detectives" and there was a wave of applause. And Morty jumped up and hugged me, and I pried myself away from him and stumbled up onto the stage. There were all of these lights shining, and everyone was applauding, and cheering, and I really felt ... I felt ...

FARRAH. Proud?

TONY. ... No ...

FARRAH. Exhilarated?

TONY. ... Loved.

FARRAH. Loved?

TONY. That's what it felt like.

(*Beat.*)

FARRAH. Jesus. (*Beat.*) What a trip.

(*TONY looks down at the carpet.*)

FARRAH. What's the matter? You won, man! What's your problem? You should be psyched!

TONY. I won for "Model Detectives."

FARRAH. Would you stop ragging on "Model Detectives"? I told you it was my favorite fucking show!— I was lying, of course.

TONY. You were lying?

FARRAH. Yeah. I like that show, "Simple Miracles," starring the guy without any arms and legs.

TONY. You like that show?

FARRAH. Yeah! I mean, the guy actually doesn't have any arms and legs. You gotta love it.

TONY. So I guess if he was just a head, you'd really love it.

FARRAH. Don't be gross. Anyway, the point is, stop moaning about your show. It's pretty good! It could be better, but it's pretty good! You're a little heavy on the laugh track sometimes, but it's your first season. You'll be able to perfect it over the next four or five years.

TONY. Four or five years—

FARRAH. Oh, cut the crap. You love it. Get over it.

TONY. I love it?

FARRAH. You love it. I want you to say it. "I Love 'Model Detectives.' " Say it.

TONY. I will not say it.

FARRAH. Say it. Or I'll grab your nuts and squeeze.

TONY. Alright, I'll say it. (*Pause.*) I can't.

FARRAH. You can. Just say it.

TONY. I ... I love "Model Detectives."

FARRAH. With feeling.

TONY. I love "Model Detectives." I love it. I love the shit.

FARRAH. Feels good, doesn't it?

TONY. Un-hunh.

FARRAH. Okay, now shut the fuck up about it, I'm sick of hearing about this stupid show.

(THEY sit there.)

TONY. We're perfect for each other.

FARRAH. Excuse me?

TONY. Nothing. I was becoming delusional for a second.

FARRAH. Yeah, I think you were. (*Beat.*) Well, think I'll go rearrange my room.

(FARRAH exits. TONY goes to his Strat-o-matic game, and puts it away. Then HE picks up the remote, and turns on the TV. HE flips from channel to channel, the VOLUME RISING, his face becoming set, hard, as the LIGHTS FADE TO BLACK.)

PROPERTY LIST

PRESET:

Ice bucket with ice
4 Glasses
Bottles of scotch, bourbon, vodka, brandy, mineral water
Strat-o-matic baseball game
Message pad and pen
Phone handset and answering machine
2 Remote controls
Ashtray and lighter
Baseball bat
Red bowl with olives
Napkin holder and napkins
Sugar bowl
Salt shaker
Lynn's clutch purse
Gourd (art object)
Lynn's suitcase
L.A. TIMES
Earrings in box
Farrah's duffel bag
Farrah's backpack with albums, lipstick, clothes
Jonny's plastic bag with clothes
Jeff's seltzer bottle
Cocaine vial
Bottle of Jack Daniels
Mineral water
2 Bottles of Bass beer
Glass of ice
People's Most Popular Award

Cereal bowl with spoon
Jeff's flowered shirt
Marlboros and matches

PERSONAL PROPS:

Business cards in holder (Tony)
Wallet with $100 (Tony)
$20 bill (Tony)
Earrings (Lynn)
Flowers in a box (Tony)

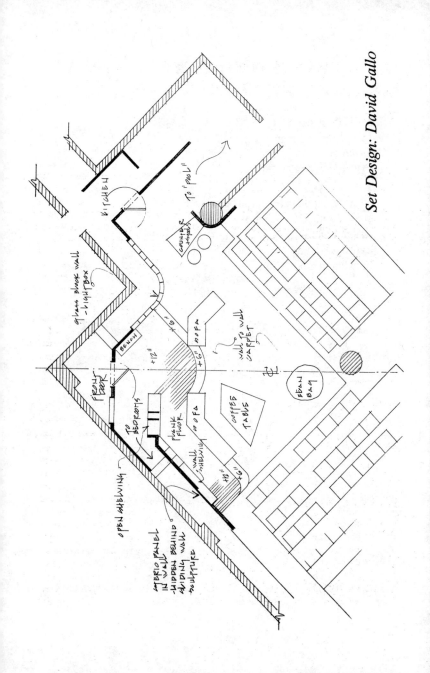

Set Design: David Gallo